Editor
Lorin Klistoff, M.A.

Managing Editor
Karen Goldfluss, M.S. Ed.

Editor-in-Chief
Sharon Coan, M.S. Ed.

Cover Artist
Lesley Palmer

Art Coordinator
Kevin Barnes

Art Director
CJae Froshay

Imaging
Ralph Olmedo, Jr.

Product Manager
Phil Garcia

Publishers
Rachelle Cracchiolo, M.S. Ed.
Mary Dupuy Smith, M.S. Ed.

Literat Circles

The Way to Go and How to Get There

Authors

Brooke Morris, M.A. and Deborah Perlenfein, M.A.

Teacher Created Materials, Inc.
6421 Industry Way
Westminster, CA 92683
www.teachercreated.com.

ISBN-0-7439-3280-3

©2003 Teacher Created Materials, Inc.

Made in U.S.A.

Table of Contents

What are literature circles?

SECTION 1

Introduction

Are you frustrated trying to match student interest with the range of reading skills and ability levels in your class? Do your students lack responsibility and ownership of their learning? Are you always looking for new ways to help students apply reading comprehension skills? Do your students need to become independent critical thinkers and enthusiastic about reading? An effective method of addressing all of these issues is to make use of literature circles.

Literature circles are student-led book groups that develop students' ownership and responsibility for their learning. Teachers can facilitate the learning by becoming a contributing member of the group and/or an outside observer that guides the process.

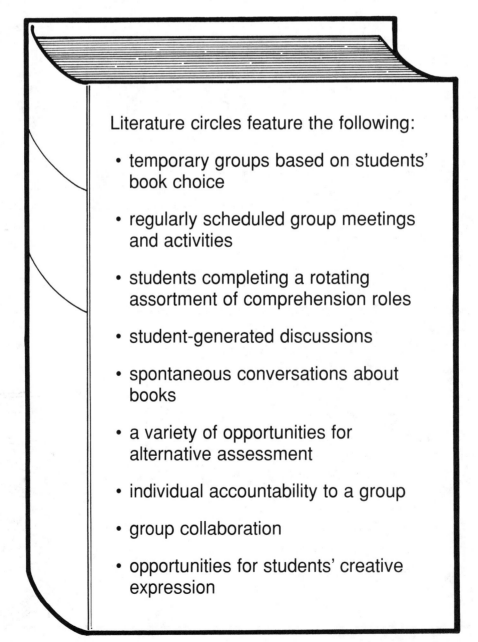

Literature circles feature the following:

- temporary groups based on students' book choice

- regularly scheduled group meetings and activities

- students completing a rotating assortment of comprehension roles

- student-generated discussions

- spontaneous conversations about books

- a variety of opportunities for alternative assessment

- individual accountability to a group

- group collaboration

- opportunities for students' creative expression

4

What Does Research Say?

Below are some examples of what researchers say about literature circles.

Literature Circles: Voice and Choice in the Student-Centered Classroom by Harvey Daniels (1994)

- "If kids never practice digging big ideas out of text themselves and always have teachers doing it for them, how can they ever achieve literary and intellectual independence?"

- "You can have a very diverse class of kids, with widely mixed ability levels, assorted cultural and ethnic identities, even lots of mainstreamed special education children, and still have an exciting, challenging, orderly, and caring atmosphere for everyone."

Methods that Matter: Six Structures for Best Practice Classrooms by Harvey Daniels and Marilyn Bizar (1998)

- "Students already get plenty of dog-eat-dog contention in school; now they need more chances to work in small teams with common purposes—just like adults do everyday, in their offices, law firms, gas stations, departments, insurance agencies, grocery stores, city councils, and ad agencies."

Tell Me: Children, Reading, and Talk by Aidan Chambers (1996)

- "Reducing literary study to a kind of multiple choice exercise with the teacher as the final answer leads kids to distrust their own experiences of the text and they report as their own the kind of responses they sense the teacher wants to hear."

Literature Study Circles in a Multicultural Classroom by K.D. Samway and Gail Whang (1996)

- "If there is anything we have learned from the students' evaluations of literature study circles, it is that they all prize discussions. To deny a student access to these rich times of sharing because of a lack of fluency as a reader is counterproductive."

Invitations: Changing as Teachers and Learners K-12 by Regie Routman (1991)

- "Perhaps most significant, literature has the power to help develop students as critical readers, writers, and thinkers. As adults, these are the people who read with questions in mind, substantiate their opinions, take an intelligent stand on an issue, read the newspaper analytically, question politicians' jargon . . ."

What Do Teachers Say?

Below is a list of questions that teachers frequently ask about literature circles.

1. **Some of my students still need other skills. How do I work that in?**

   Literature circles are only one part of a complete reading program. Like any other reading program, time is needed for skill development. As illustrated on the Sample Lesson Schedule (page 16), components of literature circles can be incorporated into the daily schedule on alternate days. The other days can be used for skill development, covering specific proficiency strands, etc. Literature circles are very flexible and can accommodate many different types of schedules.

2. **How do I accommodate for various levels within my class?**

   This will depend on the ability range of your students and the type of support that is needed. Literature circles can consist of heterogeneous or homogeneous groupings. Homogeneous groups with students of lower ability may require more teacher direction, just as any immature heterogeneous group. Homogeneous groups provide great modeling from more capable students to the student that is more challenged in reading. Many of the roles (See pages 76–78.) can be modified, done orally, or completed with the use of technology.

   Even though the text may be difficult to read, students may still be able to understand the story line and engage in discussion groups further exposing them to higher-level thinking skills. Having the passages on a tape recorder or allowing a peer or parent to read books, chapters, or specific reading assignments aloud to a student are other options. These passages can also be previewed or reviewed as needed. Alternate days in the schedule could be used to focus on specific skill development of the lower-level readers.

3. **How do I assess students in literature circles?**

   Before deciding on an assessment tool, it is always a good idea to know what is being assessed. Is the student's enjoyment of reading, reading fluency, or overall reading comprehension being assessed? All of these can be done in various ways.

   Running records can be done on individual students during group times to assess fluency, accuracy, and comprehension. Anecdotal records can be kept to note student participation in group projects and discussion. The roles that are provided run the range of higher-level thinking skills and can easily be used to assess a student's understanding of the text.

4. **We are expected to meet district and state standards (i.e., proficiency tests, district benchmarks, etc.). How do I know I will be meeting those objectives?**

   As mentioned above, the roles and classroom activities encompass a range of critical thinking skills. Specific skills are taught on alternating days or whatever schedule is determined to best fit the needs of the students. Because of the combination of direct skill instruction, higher-level skill activities, and cooperative learning (as well as culminating activities and curriculum integration), the expectations and standards of most districts and states are covered.

What Do Teachers Say? *(cont.)*

Below is an example of how the roles (pages 76–78) tie into the McREL language arts standards stated in *Content Knowledge: A Compendium of Standards and Benchmarks for K–12 Education.*

Literature Roles and Activities	McREL Standards
Connection Maker Illustrator Memory Maker News Reporter Perfect Puzzler Poetic Perceptions Read-Aloud Master Scene Setter Sequencer Summarizer Timeliner Map Matters Word Webs Word Wizard	**Standard 1:** Uses the general skills and strategies of the writing process Level II, benchmark 11 • Writes in response to literature **Standard 5:** Uses the general skills and strategies of the reading process Level II, benchmark 4, 5, 6, 7 • Makes, confirms, and revises simple predictions about what will be found in a text • Uses phonetic and structural analysis techniques, syntactic structure, and semantic context to decode unknown words • Uses a variety of context clues to decode unknown words • Uses word reference materials (e.g., glossary, dictionary, thesaurus) to determine the meaning, pronunciation, and derivations of unknown words **Standard 6:** Uses reading skills and strategies to understand and interpret a variety of literary texts Level II, benchmark 1 • Uses reading skills and strategies to understand a variety of literary passages and texts (e.g., fiction, nonfiction) **Standard 7:** Uses reading skills and strategies to understand and interpret a variety of informational texts Level II, benchmark 5 • Summarizes and paraphrases information in texts (e.g., includes the main idea and significant supporting details of a reading selection)
Advice Columnist Character Profile Commentator Connection Maker Discussion Leader Dream Weaver Efficient Effector Fortune Teller New Narrator News Reporter Poetic Perceptions Problem Solver Read-Aloud Master Scene Setter Sequencer Summarizer	**Standard 4:** Gathers and uses information for research purposes Level II, benchmarks 2, 3, 5 • Uses encyclopedias to gather information for research topics • Uses dictionaries to gather information for research topics • Uses key words, guide words, alphabetical and numerical order, indexes, cross-references, and letters on volumes to find information for research topics **Standard 5:** Uses the general skills and strategies of the reading process Level II, benchmark 4 • Makes, confirms, and revises simple predictions about what will be found in a text **Standard 6:** Uses reading skills and strategies to understand and interpret a variety of literary texts Level II, benchmarks 3, 4, 6 • Understands the basic concept of plot • Understands similarities and differences within and among literary works from various genre and cultures • Makes inferences or draws conclusions about characters' qualities and actions **Standard 7:** Uses reading skills and strategies to understand and interpret a variety of informational texts Level II, benchmark 1 • Uses reading skills and strategies to understand a variety of informational texts

What Do Students Say?

Below are actual responses from students when asked for their opinions in a Round Table Discussion lesson.

- "The thing that I like about literature circles is that they're fun, you get to work with other people, you get to read books, and then you get to write about them." —A.W.

- "If you don't understand something about the book, you can ask your group." —Stephen

- "Literature circles help me improve my understanding of the books we read. It's helpful to be able to discuss the book with peers and see what others think. Literature circles help me a lot, and they're a lot of fun." —L.C.

- "I like most of the roles; some are confusing and too long, but others are fun and help you understand words, actions, or parts/events that happened." —Brian

- "Literature circles help me to understand the book a lot better because when we do roles and share our roles, we can give a better opinion to other group members. Literature circles also help me understand a book better because I can 'summarize' the book in many different ways (roles)." —Vishi

- "I love reading out loud with my group. I also love how we do roles because that makes it fun to discuss instead of just talking. I like picking out my book to read. I love just about everything." —Whitney

- "The thing I like most is picking our own books, having roles, and forming our own groups. I like many more things about literature circles. They are so-o-o-o-o fun to do." —Trisha

What Do Students Say? *(cont.)*

- "I think discussions with other people with different opinions help you understand the meaning more clearly." —M.A.C.

- "What I like about literature circles is that we get to pick our own books, how much time we get to read in class, the types of books we have been reading recently, the roles that we do about our books, and all the time we meet." —Brian

- "It helps me understand more about what is really happening, and if I didn't understand a part we always discuss what happened, and the roles we do help also when we talk about the parts, such as Discussion Leader and the others." —Brianna

- "It improves my understanding by arguing. You can see all of the points of view, instead of just one." —Raehan

- "In literature circles I like that we can choose our own books, reading, pages, work sheets, and how long we get to read." —J.A.

- "Literature circles improve my understanding in two ways: (1) The work sheets help me understand what I read. (2) Meetings in literature circles help me understand different points of view." —S.S.

Bloom's Taxonomy

Literature circle activities offer the full range of thinking skills based on Bloom's Taxonomy. The goal of literature circles is to develop an appreciation for literature, author's style, and purpose and for assessing individual tastes. Roles that are linked to Bloom's Taxonomy help provide students with activities that cover the full range of thinking skills to meet and reach above their cognitive abilities.

Step 1: Knowledge	Role Correlations
These roles require students to recall basic facts about the selection. Information for these activities are right within the text and can be easily found. Students should be able to do the following: • match • identify • list • arrange • recall	All roles require a higher level of thinking than this—except for the first level of questioning on the Discussion Leader.
Step 2: Comprehension	**Role Correlations**
Similar to Step 1 (Knowledge), these roles require students to take their knowledge of the selection and demonstrate a basic understanding of its contents. Students should be able to do the following: • interpret • explain • draw • predict • construct	• Circle Sequencer • Efficient Effector • Fortune Teller • Map Matters • Perfect Puzzler • Problem Solver • Sequencer • Summarizer • Scene Setter

Sample prompts for knowledge and comprehension may include the following:

- Define the meaning of . . .
- List as many . . .
- Name as many . . .

- Retell the key events when . . .
- Describe in your own words . . .
- What was the solution to the problem?

Bloom's Taxonomy *(cont.)*

Step 3: Application	Role Correlations
Activities at this level require students to make new use of the information they have gained through reading the selection. Students should be able to do the following: • classify • transfer • make • select • think • give	• Character Connections • Character Web • Connection Maker • Emotional Events • Poetic Perceptions • Sensational Sequels • Word Webs • Word Wizard
Step 4: Analysis	**Role Correlations**
Activities at this level ask students to relate the parts to the whole. Parts of the selection are examined closely to better understand the overall story. Students should be able to do the following: • identify • distinguish • select • differentiate • compare and/or contrast	• A Time of Change • Character Profile • Commentator • Illustrator • Meeting of the Minds • Read-Aloud Master • Point/Counterpoint • Trait Tracker

Sample prompts for application and analysis may include the following:

- Compare/Contrast the main view point of . . .
- Investigate some alternative ways the character . . .
- Illustrate with words and pictures your ideas about . . .

- Classify the characters with the characteristics of . . .
- How can you make use of . . .
- How can you solve . . .
- Choose the . . .

Bloom's Taxonomy *(cont.)*

Step 5: Synthesis	Role Correlations
Roles at this level require students to take different parts of the story and put them together in a new way to form a unique product or idea. Students should be able to do the following: • write • create • restructure • compose • imagine	• Advice Columnist • Dream Weaver • Memory Maker • New Narrator • Meaningful Mottos • News Reporter • Timeliner • "Wanted!" Poster
Step 6: Evaluation	**Role Correlations**
Students are asked at this level to form an opinion about the selection and be able to support it with sound evidence and reasoning. Students should be able to do the following: • decide • judge • consider • appraise • compare • write	• A Sense of Character • Discussion Leader (*Note:* Many roles contain an element of this where students offer supporting thoughts and opinions while identifying the text as evidence.)

Sample prompts for synthesis and evaluation may include the following:

• What would happen if . . .
• How would you improve . . .
• Determine what would happen if . . .
• Decide what would happen if there were . . .

• Assess how you would feel if . . .
• Imagine how . . .
• Predict what would happen if . . .
• Can you prove that . . .

How do I manage and organize literature circles?

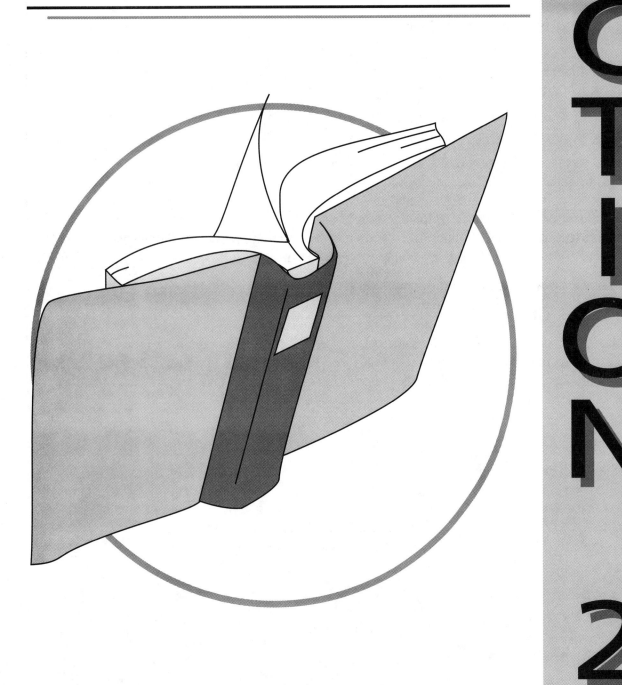

The Progression of Literature Circle Lessons

The following is a framework for preparing students to run independent groups. The progression of each step is dependent on the skill, ability, and maturity of the class, as well as the teacher's willingness to be a facilitator/coach instead of a dispenser of information.

Step 1: Class Read Aloud

A. Books—The teacher selects one title to be read by the entire class. The teacher controls the pace that the students move through the book. Titles can be selected in conjunction with a thematic unit, content area studies, genre, author study, etc.

B. Groups—The class functions as one literature circle. The teacher's role is to model the appropriate expectations, behavior, participation, and responsibility.

C. Roles—At this level, key roles are introduced and taught. The entire class is assigned the same role at the same time over the same reading selection. As a group, students share the role with the group while the teacher models and critiques their efforts. A suggested progression of roles would be 1) Illustrator, 2) Sequencer, 3) Read-Aloud Master, 4) Scene Setter, 5) Discussion Leader, 6) Connection Maker, and 7) Summarizer. The order of the remaining roles can be based on the skill the teacher needs to emphasize, for example using Commentator to focus on fact and opinion concepts.

Step 2: Small Groups (Same Book)

A. Books—Each group is assigned the same book. The teacher controls the pace in which all groups move through the book. The teacher may want to offer a variety of books and allow for the class to vote on which is used for each of the small groups. Students change groups each time a new book is studied.

B. Groups—Each group has the responsibility as modeled in the large group. The teacher monitors group progress and advises the groups on specific concerns.

C. Roles—Each group member is assigned a different role for predetermined sections in the book. When groups meet, each member is responsible for sharing his or her work. It is suggested that the roles used in the first round of small groups be the same as those introduced in the Class Read Aloud.

14

The Progression of Literature Circle Lessons *(cont.)*

Step 3: Small Groups (Different Books Assigned)

A. Books—Each group is assigned a different book by the teacher. Initially the teacher may opt to create groups by ability level for management concerns, but later it is important to move into heterogeneous grouping.

B. Groups—Cooperatively, each group is self-paced. The teacher continues to guide them through the process, take anecdotal records, check assignments, and offer suggestions to the group. The groups become more independent in conducting the discussion and sharing of roles. The teacher introduces the assignment calendar (page 20) as a means to guide students to plan their reading and roles weekly.

C. Roles—As in the previous grouping, the students take on different roles for each predetermined section of the book. The choice of roles can be expanded to meet curriculum objectives of the teacher. (*Note:* New roles should be introduced and modeled to the whole class before adding them as options in the assignments for group members.)

Step 4: Independent Groups—Student Book Choice/Assignment Calendars (The Ultimate Goal)

This is the last step in group autonomy. At this point, students have learned the process and expectations of literature circles and have been successful. Students are expected to take ownership and control of their own learning. (*Note:* There may be only one or two groups in a class that are ready for this step. It may even be more manageable for the teacher to start off with only one group taking on this responsibility.)

A. Books—The teacher presents a variety of books and allows the students to select the top three that they would like to read. The teacher forms the groups based on student choices. This allows for some teacher control. Books offered can vary in difficulty and length while still focusing on a theme, content area, genre, etc.

B. Groups—Groups remain self-paced by using the assignment calendar and following the daily and weekly routines.

C. Roles—Group members are responsible for gathering, assigning, and completing roles according to teacher expectations.

Sample Lesson Schedule

Monday	Tuesday	Wednesday	Thursday	Friday
Literature Circles **Mini Lesson** • Introduce and model the reading strategy for the week. (See pages 94–101.) • Introduce corresponding role sheet. **Group Meeting** • Groups discuss weekend reading. • Groups assign reading and roles to each member and plan the calendar (page 20).	**Reading Lab** • Have independent reading and time to work on role sheets. • Have teacher conferences.	**Literature Circles** **Group Meeting** • Groups discuss and share completed roles. • Groups plan the calendar for the next assignment. • Students read as a group or with a buddy. **Book Lover's Journal** • Students complete journal entry in class or as an assignment. (See page 87.)	**Reading Strategies** **Mini-Lesson** • Practice reading strategy introduced on Monday. • Apply the strategy to nonfiction reading, such as a *Teen Newsweek* article.	**Literature Circles** **Fish Bowl** • See page 105 for Fish Bowl directions. **Round Table Discussions** • See page 106 for directions on Round Table Discussions. **Group Meeting** • Groups discuss and share completed roles or journal entries. • Groups assign weekend reading.

Teacher Responsibilities

Before Implementing Literature Circles

It is recommended that the teacher set up a daily/weekly schedule prior to implementing literature circles. Page 16 shows just one sample. Students tend to feel a sense of security with a schedule; they know what to expect, and it can keep them on track with their assignments. This schedule can change until one is created that is comfortable for the teacher and students.

- As literature circles evolve into more independent work groups, developing a personal organizational scheme for handing out and receiving paperwork is a must. It may be helpful for each group to have a folder where role sheets are kept for the group. Anecdotal notes and their assignment sheet may also be kept in this folder. Students can become independent in refilling their role sheets. The teacher should predetermine which role sheets will be the focus and have a supply available in a convenient area for students to access.

- Outline a yearly plan based on themes, content area, or core curriculum. If themes are used, decide what groups of books will be introduced with each theme. Students may progress through one or several books during each theme, depending on the book and student ability. Sample themes and book lists are offered on pages 127–136.

- Organize the classroom, books, and role sheets. For example, set desks in groups, have a common place for turning in papers, set up a filing system for role sheets that is accessible to students (hanging file folder), have a clipboard for anecdotal notes, have a place to hang sample papers, journals, etc.

- Set expectations for student calendar assignments (i.e., number of pages to read, number of roles to complete each week, when each role is due, reading log if being used, etc.).

- Pre-read all books. Keep a teacher copy with notes to prepare kids, to engage in group conversations, to answer questions, etc.

- Develop consequences for inappropriate behavior, being frequently unprepared, or absent from the group. One quick method is "three strikes you are out"; the student must read independently and must complete book reports, and summaries, in addition to the role sheets they would be doing with the group. The student can rejoin at the beginning of the next unit.

Teacher Responsibilities *(cont.)*

During Literature Circles

- Take anecdotal notes, brief observations, on computer labels to give to each group regarding progress, cooperation, and areas to improve upon. Always try to include positive comments with every suggestion for improvement.
- Keep a set of teacher notes concerning positive and negative student behavior, ideas for new roles, skills to be reviewed, roles to reflect upon, and modifications needed.
- Meet with a group as an observer or as an active participant, depending on the needs of the group.
- Pull an individual student during group reading times to do reading inventories or running records.
- Collect completed role sheets, daily reports, chapter reviews, and book lover journals.

After Literature Circles

- Examine the role sheets to assess individual learning, group learning, and progress. Use student samples as models on an overhead to show how to improve future work.
- Develop modifications or enrichment activities, depending on student needs.
- Adjust schedules, depending on the quality of the work received. If students need to review a concept, the same role may need to be repeated.
- Review anecdotal notes to plan for future lessons.
- Showcase student work and share with other teachers.
- Continue professional development on literature circles by reading current literature. (See Bibliography on page 144.)

Friendly Reminders

- Remember, developing literature circles is a progression of student skills, ability, and responsibility.
- Personalize the program as needed. Your literature circles may be different from year to year, based on student skills, ability, and background with literature circles.
- Some classes may not progress through all four levels of literature circle development—that is fine!
- Comprehension occurs when students are given the opportunity to create their own meaning and connections.
- As much as you may want to intervene, allow the students to lead their own discussions.
- Create a literature format that works for your classroom and the needs of the students. What you want to do may not be what works best for that particular class.
- Organization and format may vary from year to year. Change is good!

18

Student Responsibilities

Before Class

- Read the assigned selection.

- Complete roles.

- Be prepared for group discussion.

During Literature Circles

- Gather group folder and other materials.

- Share roles and add to group discussion.

- Remember the following discussion elements:

  - Focus on discussion.

  - Listen actively.

  - Actively participate.

  - Piggyback off others' ideas.

  - Ask questions for clarification.

  - Disagree constructively.

  - Take turns to let others speak.

  - Support opinions with evidence.

  - Encourage others.

- Assign reading and roles. Record on the calendar in the group folder.

- Complete required daily activities (daily report, book log, chapter reviews).

- Read aloud with the group or a buddy.

After Literature Circles

- Complete reading and assignments.

- Participate in sharing showcase, if appropriate.

- Tell others about experiences with the book.

- Read, read, read.

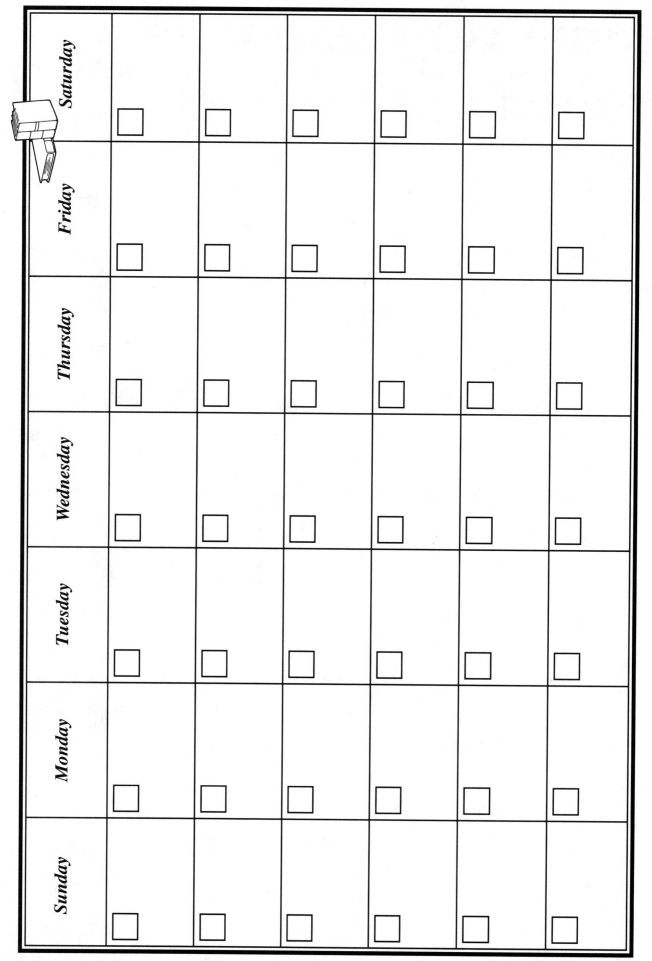

How do I use the roles?

Explanation of the Role Sheets

Literature circles are independent, temporary book groups based on students' book choice. Children read the chosen selection and then meet to discuss their understanding and reactions to the text, as well as their reactions to other members' interpretations. The discussions revolve around students' role sheets, which give a different comprehension task to each group member. The success of each group depends on the quality of the conversation facilitated through the role sheets. An example of a role sheet would be the student who is assigned the "Discussion Leader." That student must prepare an assortment of literal, inferential, and interpretive questions for the group to answer orally. The "Read-Aloud Master" must chose six significant passages to reread with the group and then discuss that selection's importance to the story.

Benefits of the Role Sheets

The following are some benefits to using the role sheets.

1. **Conversations originate from ideas on the role sheets.**

   The role sheets are not merely work sheet activities for students to complete and teachers to grade. Group members use role sheets as a catalyst for discussion. This discussion can aid in developing more breadth and depth of understanding between the reader and the text.

2. **Students have clearly defined interlocking tasks.**

   The role sheets provide a purpose for reading. Research indicates that having a purpose helps students determine what is important in the text, what is remembered, and comprehension strategies to use. When sharing role sheets in a group, the students can see the connections between the different reading strategies emphasized on the role sheets.

3. **Students make meaning after reading.**

   Once a purpose has been set and the students have read the text, then the role sheets can help them reflect on their reading and build on their understanding.

4. **Teachers have physical representation of individual learning.**

   Role sheets provide tangible evidence of students' thought processes and understanding of the text. These sheets can be kept over a period of time to show individual growth and also for assessment purposes.

5. **Students are exposed to the skills of the role sheets year-round.**

   For example, when predicting is introduced in a mini-lesson, students complete the Fortune Teller role sheet. This same sheet can be used whenever it is appropriate to the text being studied. Therefore, a student may be introduced to the role in October and use it again in January and March. The expectation is that the student retains the knowledge of that strategy and can apply it at a higher level as the year progresses.

6. **Teachers can create new roles to meet a curricular objective.**

   Any of the role sheets presented in this book can be modified to meet the needs of individual students or a particular curriculum. Any activity that is used regularly can be turned into a role for literature circles.

7. **Roles can be used for fiction and nonfiction selections.**

   Careful consideration should be used when selecting roles for nonfiction text. For example, Dream Weaver may be a difficult role to complete for nonfiction text, whereas Word Wizard would be very applicable.

Things to Remember

1. Before students are given the role sheets to complete independently, they must be familiar with the concepts of the role and know the expectations of the teacher.

2. The roles are supposed to rotate each time the group meets, so that as the students read the text they are working with different skills. Members of a group should not complete the same role over a selected reading unless you are in the beginning stages of literature circles.

3. The method of organizing the role sheets will vary with the grade level of the students. One method that has worked well in the intermediate grades is having a filing system with copies of each role in different hanging file folders. The students keep a set of the roles in their group folder, and as they complete their set, they refill with new roles. (Depending on the length of the book, students may not finish all their roles in one book. If this happens, students carry their remaining roles to their new book group.) In the primary grades, a method that has worked is to staple a set of roles in varying order for each group member. Students complete the roles in the order of their packets.

4. As new roles are introduced, teachers may rotate those roles in and filter out some of the beginning roles.

5. The one role that should always be completed by one of the group members is the Discussion Leader. This person leads the group in conversation and brings their group into discussions over critical parts. The Read-Aloud Master and Sequencer are also key roles. (Students can be allowed to complete these roles more than once before they are finished with their original set of roles.)

6. When students are participating in self-sufficient literature circles, they should have a set routine for assigning and completing roles. (See the Sample Lesson Schedule on page 16.)

7. Literature can be taught with articles, short stories, picture books, and content-area texts, as well as novels.

8. Following this section are Role Review sheets on pages 76–78 that can be copied for students to keep in their folders or journals to use as a reference when discussing roles with their group or in a teacher conference.

Action Plot-O-Graph

Group Name _____

Book _____   Author _____

Action usually occurs throughout a story. It may start out low and build, or it may start out intense and decrease. An extreme break in the action marks the *climax* of a story. For each chapter, color the bar graph to show the intensity of the action. As a group, use the other page to describe the action in each chapter, note the intensity level and the significance of the action. Use additional paper for books that include more than 10 chapters.

Climatic Action									
Great Action									
Obvious Action									
Some Action									
Low Action									
No Action									
Chapter	1	2	3	4	5	6	7	8	9	10

Action Plot-O-Graph (cont.)

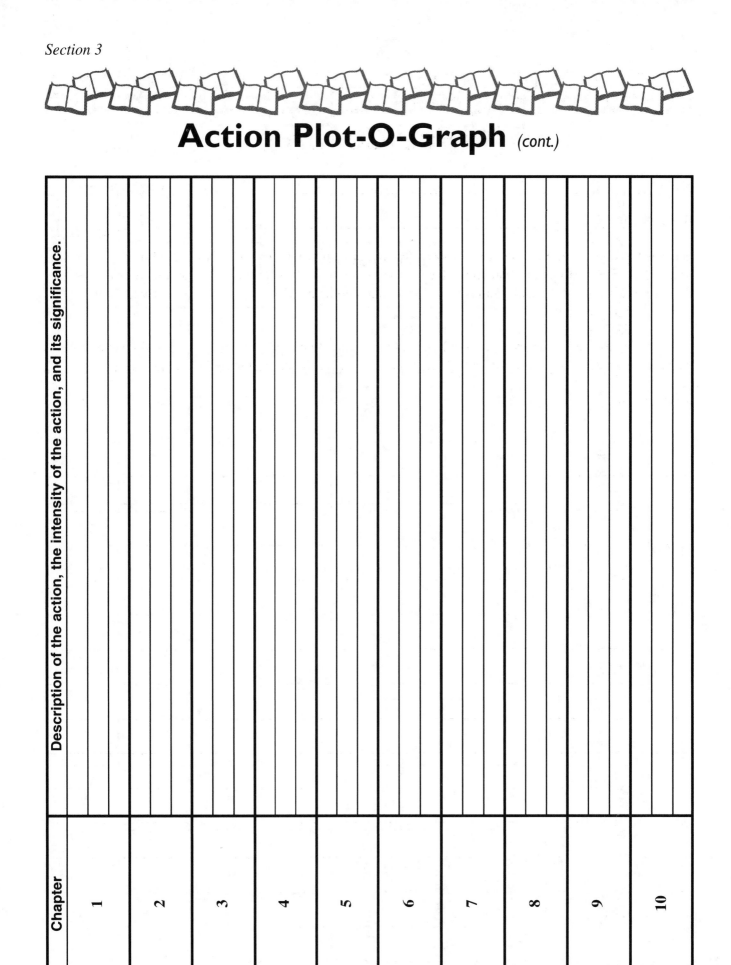

Chapter	Description of the action, the intensity of the action, and its significance.
1	
2	
3	
4	
5	
6	
7	
8	
9	
10	

Advice Columnist

Name_____

Book _____

What is the conflict in your story? Choose a character from your story who is affected by the problem or conflict. Pretend you are that character and write a letter to "Dear Abby" explaining your problem. Be sure to give accurate background knowledge and a complete description of the conflict. Don't forget to sign your letter!

Share the letter with your group by reading it aloud. On the next page, your group should write "Dear Abby's" letter back to your character. Include ideas on how the character can solve the conflict.

Dear Abby,

_____

_____

_____

_____

_____

_____

_____

_____

_____

_____

_____

_____

_____

_____

_____

_____,

_____

Advice Columnist *(cont.)*

Dear _____,

_____

_____

_____

_____

_____

_____

_____

_____

_____

_____

_____

_____

_____

_____

_____

_____

_____

_____

_____

_____

_____

Sincerely,

Abby

A Sense of Character

Name_____

Book _____

To truly understand a character in a story, you must "walk in their shoes" (that is, think as they think, and feel as they feel). Complete the diagram below to show what a character in the story thinks, feels, smells, hears, loves, does, and where they go to give us a total sense of that character. Find quotes in the book to show how the author provided evidence of these traits. On the back of the paper, briefly discuss how the senses of the character are similar or different from you.

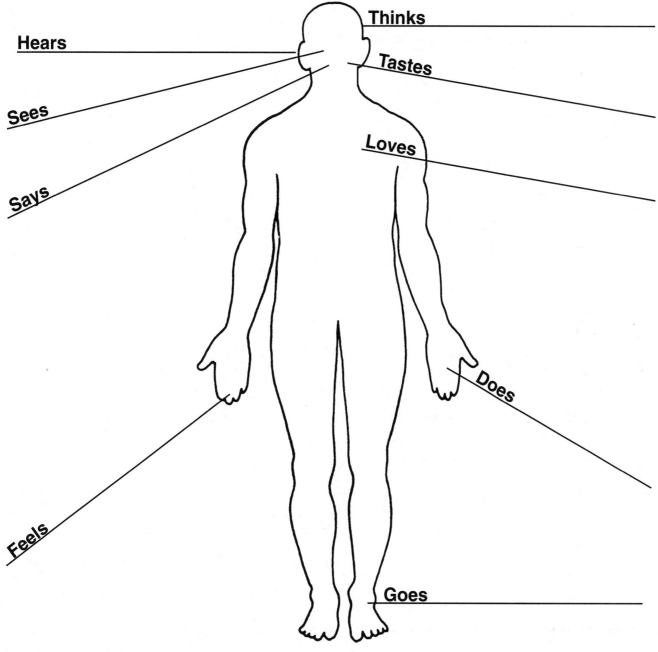

Thinks _____

Hears _____

Tastes _____

Sees _____

Loves _____

Says _____

Does _____

Feels _____

Goes _____

A Time of Change

Name _____

Book _____

We all grow as people from the experiences that we have in our lives. Sometimes we learn valuable lessons that can change our lives, beliefs, and actions. The characters in stories we read change as well. Think of a character in the story and the experiences they had. Explain the lessons they learned that changed them as a person.

I. Character: _____

    A. Events or experiences this character had

       _____

       _____

       _____

    B. Lessons this character learned

       _____

       _____

       _____

    C. Ways this character changed

       _____

       _____

       _____

II. What did you learn from the story? How might that help you change as a person?

_____

_____

_____

_____

_____

Character Connections

Name _____

Book _____

Think of all the different characters in the story and the connections you can make with them. On the left side, complete the sentence with the name of a character in the story. On the right side, give a brief explanation of how or why you connect, or identify, with that character.

Name of Character	Explanation
I most admire _____ .	
I mostly dislike _____ .	
I would most likely be a friend to _____ _____ .	
I could learn the most from _____ .	
I would enjoy another book about _____ _____ .	
I would like to know more about _____ _____ .	

Character Profile

Name _____

Book _____

Develop one of the main characters in the story into a real person. Try to use the information from the book. Don't reveal the name of the character; let the group guess based on the clues you tell them. As another option, tell the group the character and have them give suggestions for the profile.

Name of Character: _____

Age: _____   Height: _____   Weight: _____   Male or Female: _____

Hair Color: _____   Eye Color: _____   Skin Color: _____

Where does he or she live? _____

What kind of job does he or she have or would like to have? Why? _____

_____

Who is his or her best friend? _____

Who are his or her enemies? _____

What does he or she like most about life? _____

List his or her favorites:

Color _____   Food _____   Animal _____

Hobby _____   Sport _____   Music _____

Place to go _____

Things to do _____

Character Profile *(cont.)*

Would you like to have this person for a friend? _____

Explain why or why not.

_____

_____

_____

_____

_____

Cite some places in the book that support at least three of your responses in this character profile.

_____

_____

_____

_____

_____

_____

_____

Based on your responses, draw a picture or profile of the character.

Character Web

Name_____

Book _____

Webs show us how characters, settings, or events are related to each other. Think of the characters in the selection you just read. How are they related to the main character and to each other? They can be related not only like family, but tied together by events or feelings. Write the name of the main character and four other character's names in the clouds. Use the boxes to write a brief statement to show the connection between the characters. Add a cloud to show how you can relate with one or more of the characters.

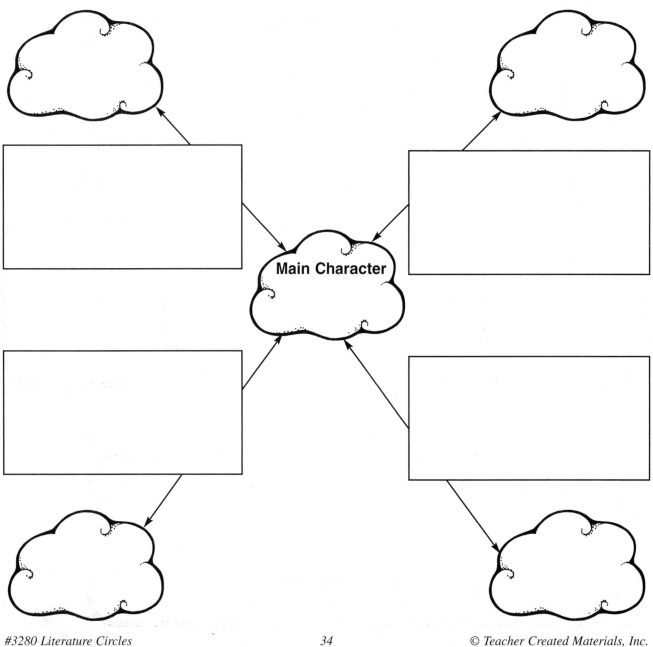

Circle Sequencer

Name_____

Book _____

The sequence of some events is a continuous process or happens in a circle ending where the action began. Some events in the story build on each other to a climax. Use the Circle Sequencer to identify the main event in the story. In the boxes, describe the events that led up to the event and/or followed the event if the main event is not the climax. Pictures may be used to illustrate the steps in the process or cycle.

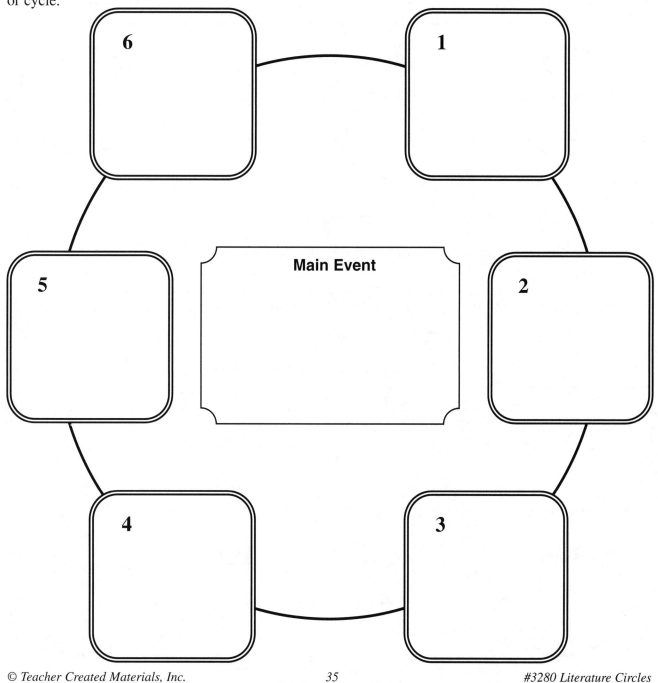

Commentator

Name _____

Book _____

Write eight statements about your reading. Include both facts and opinions. Read each statement to your group members, and let them debate whether it is a fact or opinion. Share your point of view. Remember, a **fact** is a statement that can be proven true or false. An **opinion** is a belief—it cannot be measured. An opinion uses words such as *best, worst, should, should not,* or *think.*

1. _____

   _____

   This is a(n) _____ because _____

(fact/opinion)

   _____

2. _____

   _____

   This is a(n) _____ because _____

(fact/opinion)

   _____

3. _____

   _____

   This is a(n) _____ because _____

(fact/opinion)

   _____

4. _____

   _____

   This is a(n) _____ because _____

(fact/opinion)

   _____

  36

Commentator (cont.)

5. _____

_____

This is a(n) _____ because _____
    (fact/opinion)

_____

6. _____

_____

This is a(n) _____ because _____
    (fact/opinion)

_____

7. _____

_____

This is a(n) _____ because _____
    (fact/opinion)

_____

8. _____

_____

This is a(n) _____ because _____
    (fact/opinion)

_____

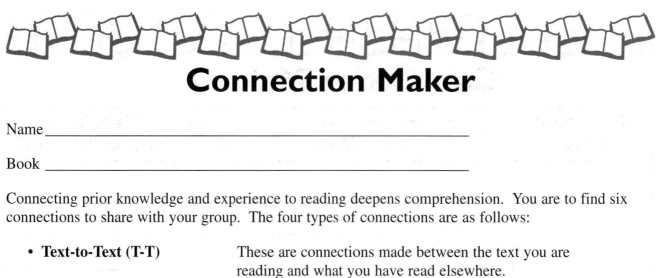

Connection Maker

Name_____

Book _____

Connecting prior knowledge and experience to reading deepens comprehension. You are to find six connections to share with your group. The four types of connections are as follows:

- **Text-to-Text (T-T)**   These are connections made between the text you are reading and what you have read elsewhere.

- **Text-to-World (T-W)**   These are connections made between the text you are reading and the bigger issues and events of the world.

- **Text-to-Self (T-S)**   These are connections made between the text you are reading and your own experiences.

- **Text-Within-Text (T-W-T)**   These are connections made between the text you are reading and another section of that same text.

Label the type of connection you are making and explain the connection. The connection codes are in parentheses above. In your connection be sure to explain both parts. This includes explaining the part of the book the connection relates to and the connection you made. When your group meets, share your connections and invite group members to each share a connection they made during the reading.

Connection Code	Explanation of the Connection Made	How did this help our understanding of the story?

Connection Maker *(cont.)*

Connection Code	Explanation of the Connection Made	How did this help our understanding of the story?

Adapted from Daniels, H. *Literature Circles: Voice and Choice in the Student-Centered Classroom.* York, ME: Stenhouse Publishers, 1994.

Discussion Leader

Name_____

Book _____

Create 12 thoughtful questions for your group to answer orally. You must create three discussion questions from each level (literal, inferential, and interpretive). You may choose from the critical question starters below, or design your own. These questions must relate to the section of the text you were assigned.

When your group meets, you facilitate the question and answer session. Be sure to encourage all group members to contribute as well as include your own thoughts. You may be asked to answer these questions in your journal.

Right There Questions (Literal Questions): The answer is right there in the story. You can point to the answer. The words used to make up the question are often the same words that are in the answer.

Define the meaning of _____

Where was _____

Name as many _____

Describe in your own words_____

What happened when _____

What are the characters doing to solve the problem of _____

Which character _____

Create your own literal questions: _____

_____

_____

_____

_____

_____

_____

Discussion Leader *(cont.)*

Think and Search (Inferential Questions): The answer is in the text, but it needs to be put together with different pieces of information from the book. You have to think and search for the answer.

How would you compare _____

Choose the best _____

How could the character _____

What is the difference between _____

Create your own inferential questions: _____

_____

_____

_____

_____

The Author and Me (Interpretive Questions): You need to think about what you know and what the author has said in the text. The answer will be from both the author and you as you infer meaning. The answer won't be found on the printed page, but the information to answer the question is there.

Predict what would happen if _____

Why did the author include _____

Can you prove that _____

What was the author's purpose when _____

What will happen when _____

Why did the character _____

Create your own interpretive questions: _____

_____

_____

_____

_____

Discussion Leader (cont.)

My Own Thoughts: The answer is not in the story. The question is asking for your own thoughts about something in the story. It can be creative or open-ended and there is no right or wrong answer, but the answer should be supported by the text and your personal experiences and beliefs.

Assess how I would feel if _____

How would I improve _____

How did I feel when _____

Why do I think_____

Was it fair when _____

Create "My Own Thoughts" questions: _____

_____

_____

_____

_____

Adapted from Daniels, H. *Literature Circles: Voice and Choice in the Student-Centered Classroom.* York, ME: Stenhouse Publishers, 1994.

Dream Weaver

Name _____

Book _____

In the area below, draw what you think a character from your book would like to dream about.

Describe why that dream has significance for that character. Cite at least two examples from the book to support your reasoning for the drawing.

_____

_____

_____

_____

_____

_____

_____

Efficient Effector

Name_____

Book _____

In a cause-and-effect relationship, one event causes another event to happen. What happens first is the cause; what happens as a result is the effect. Effects then become cause. Think about the cause-and-effect relationships in your reading. Identify the linked relationships in the spaces below. When your group meets, read the initial cause and see if your group can discover the links without you telling them. Write in complete sentences. Draw in a diagonal line to show the connection between an effect and the next cause when needed.

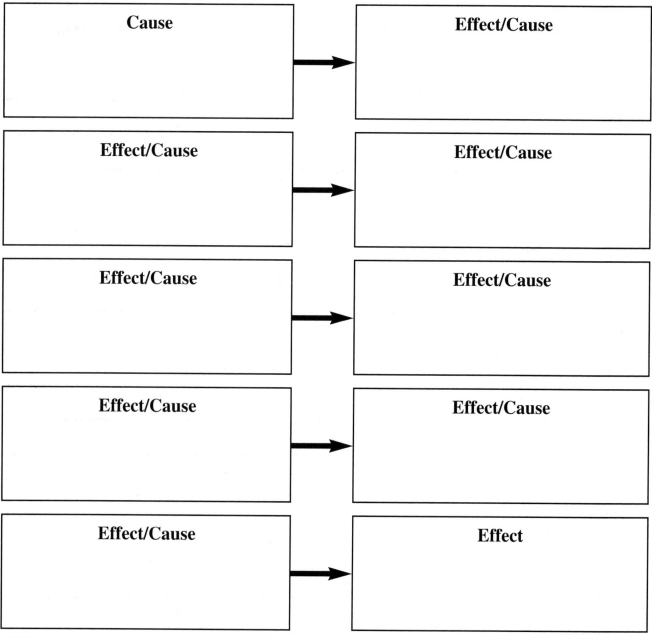

Emotional Events

Name _____

Book _____

Describe the events in the story that made you or a selected character feel the following emotions.

Surprise _____

_____

_____

Sadness _____

_____

_____

Disgust _____

_____

_____

Hopelessness _____

_____

_____

Anger _____

_____

_____

Emotional Events (cont.)

Worry

_____

_____

_____

Hope

_____

_____

_____

Fear

_____

_____

_____

Pity

_____

_____

_____

Frustration

_____

_____

_____

Joy

_____

_____

_____

46

Fortune Teller

Name _____

Book _____

Choose a character from your book and predict what that character's life will be like in the future. Base your predictions on your reading and cite examples from the book that support your predictions. Make certain that your predictions are things that could really happen to the character. Have group members share any predictions they have about other characters in the book.

Illustrator

Name _____

Book _____

On the back of this page or on a different sheet of paper, draw a picture of something that is connected specifically to your book. It can be displayed as a cartoon, chart, diagram, or a sketch. Look at the examples below.

Examples: character, setting, problem, an exciting part, a surprise, a prediction, etc.

When your group meets, do not tell what the drawing is. Let them guess and talk about it first. Then you can tell about it. Have your group title the picture. With your group, write a brief description telling the significance of the picture. Your description should explain something that can't be seen by looking at the picture. Do not just describe the picture.

Significance of the picture: _____

_____

_____

_____

_____

_____

_____

_____

_____

_____

_____

_____

_____

Adapted from Daniels, H. *Literature Circles: Voice and Choice in the Student-Centered Classroom.* York, ME: Stenhouse Publishers, 1994.

Map Matters

Name _____

Book _____

In the space below draw a map of the places where events occurred in the selection. Label when and where important events happened. Remember, a setting may be within a building, city, country, or whole continent.

Meaningful Mottos

Name _____

Book _____

A *motto* is a word or phrase that describes a principle that someone lives by or believes in. For example, "To thine own self be true"; "Haste makes waste"; or "Do not judge a person until you have walked a mile in his moccasins."

> **"To read or not to read, that is the question."**
>
> **Teacher**

Create a motto for four characters in the story. Write the motto in the top section of the banner. When your group meets, share the mottos with them and see if they can determine which motto goes with which character. Write the name in the bottom section of the banner. Let the group help develop a sentence as to why it is a good motto for that character. Write the sentence below the banner.

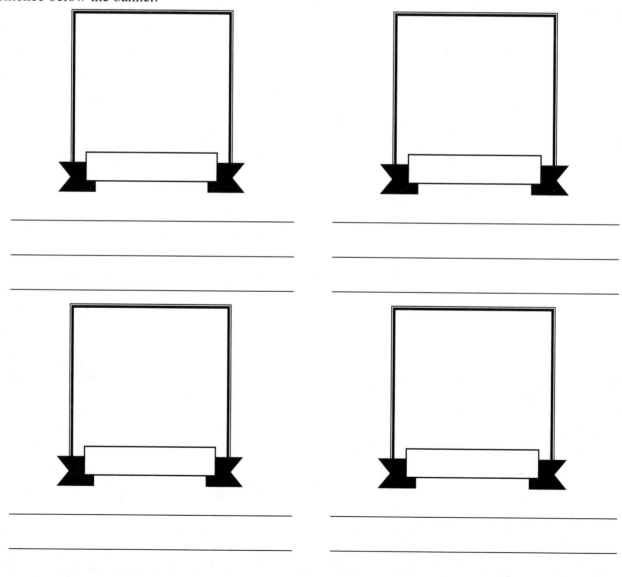

Meeting of the Minds

Name _____

Book _____

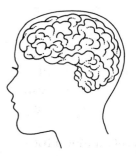

Often characters in a story have a conflict or disagree about an issue. Think of two characters in the story that you just read. Identify the issue or conflict between the two characters. Label each profile with the character's name. Restate each character's point of view and how he or she changed to reach an agreement. At the bottom explain how the conflict was resolved.

Issue: _____	
Character: _____	**Character:** _____
View Point: _____ _____ _____ _____ _____ _____ _____ _____ _____	**View Point:** _____ _____ _____ _____ _____ _____ _____ _____
Resolution: _____ _____ _____ _____	

Memory Maker

Name _____

Book _____

Think about items that are very important to a character or characters in your book. Select at least five items to create a scrapbook page that contains pictures and mementos that represent significant things for the character(s). Draw a picture of each item and include a two- to three-sentence explanation next to each one. Use sheets of paper to make your scrapbook. You may use this page to brainstorm your ideas. Be creative!

Name of Character(s): _____

Ideas

1. _____

_____

2. _____

_____

3. _____

_____

4. _____

_____

5. _____

_____

6. _____

_____

7. _____

_____

8. _____

_____

New Narrator

Name_____

Book _____

Think about who the narrator is in your story. Most stories are told from the main character's point of view. Choose a minor character from your book and retell a scene from that character's viewpoint. Read it to your group and have them guess the narrator.

New Narrator:_____

New Narrator's Viewpoint: _____

_____

_____

_____

_____

_____

_____

_____

_____

_____

_____

_____

_____

_____

_____

_____

News Reporter

Name_____

Book _____

Write a newspaper article about an event that occurred during your reading. Remember that newspaper journalists try to answer the following questions: *who, what, where, when,* and *why.* Answer the questions below and then use the responses to write the article on the next page. Add a catchy headline. Share your article with your group.

Who? _____

_____

_____

What? _____

_____

_____

Where?_____

_____

_____

When? _____

_____

_____

Why? _____

_____

_____

_____

News Reporter (cont.)

_____

(headline)

by _____

Perfect Puzzler

Name _____

Book _____

Create a word puzzle with 15 vocabulary words for you and your group.
The puzzle you create can be done on the computer or with paper and
pencil. Use the following guidelines:

- Make enough copies of your puzzle to pass out to your group, for
  yourself, and to turn in with this page.
- You may create a secret code puzzle, a crossword, word search, etc.
- Use words from the assignment that you may not know, have not heard, or that are not used very
  often.
- Your puzzle may contain word lists as a reference or sentences and definitions as hints.
- On this paper, list the words you will use in your puzzle and the page number on which they are
  found.

Vocabulary Words	Page Number
1.	
2.	
3.	
4.	
5.	
6.	
7.	
8.	
9.	
10.	
11.	
12.	
13.	
14.	
15.	

Poetic Perceptions

Name_____

Book _____

Create a poem about a character in the book. Write the poem in the format presented below and base it on what you have learned about this character in the book. Add your words to the blank lines. Center the poem on your paper as it appears in the box and leave out the line numbering and italic words. If you would rather, you may choose to create your own poem based on a character.

When your group meets, read your poem aloud. On the back of the poem, your group should write three positive comments and two suggestions regarding the content of your poem.

Line 1: _____ *(first name of character)*

Line 2: _____ , _____ , _____ , _____ *(four traits that describe him or her)*

Line 3: Relative of _____ *(father, sister, daughter, teacher, inventor)*

Line 4: Lover of _____ , _____ , _____ *(list three things or people)*

Line 5: Who feels _____ , _____ , _____ *(list three emotions)*

Line 6: Who needs _____ , _____ , _____ *(list three items)*

Line 7: Who fears _____ , _____ , _____ *(list three items)*

Line 8: Who gives _____ , _____ , _____ *(list three items)*

Line 9: Who would like to see _____ , _____ , _____ *(list three changes or places)*

Line 10: Resident of _____ *(where he or she lived)*

Line 11: _____ *(last name of character)*

Point/Counterpoint

Name _____

Book _____

There are times when we disagree with the thoughts or actions of a character in a story. Think about a character in the story you just read. What did they do, think, or feel that you disagree with and would have done differently. Explain the character's point of view on the left side and your counter point of view on the right side. At the bottom describe what you would have done differently. How would this have changed the story?

_____ **Point of View** *(Character's Name)*	**My Point of View**
_____ _____ _____ _____ _____ _____ _____	_____ _____ _____ _____ _____ _____ _____

What I would have done is _____

_____

_____

The story would change in that _____

_____

_____

Power Graph

Group Name _____

Book _____

Select two main characters to chart throughout the story. Write their names at the bottom of the graph and indicate the color that will represent them on the graph. For each chapter, mark the section of the graph that shows the power of each character (1 = low power, 10 = most power). Power can be the intensity, prominence, or influence of the characters' role in that chapter or it could be the power the character has during specific events of that chapter. As a group, write a brief description explaining the placements on the graph. At the end of the book, write about the patterns noticed in the graph. Did the roles change for the characters? How did it match with events in the story? Attach all work.

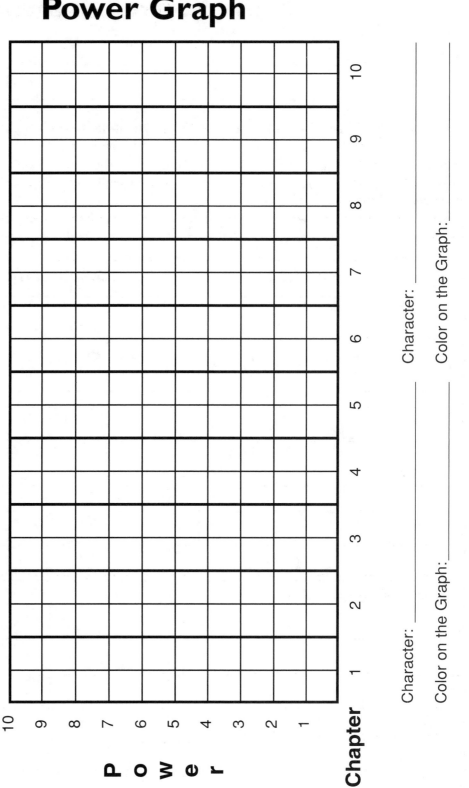

P
o
w
e
r

10 9 8 7 6 5 4 3 2 1

Chapter 1 2 3 4 5 6 7 8 9 10

Character: _____

Color on the Graph: _____

Character: _____

Color on the Graph: _____

Problem Solver

Name_____

Book _____

Every story has a basic problem or conflict. Throughout the story there are minor conflicts that the characters experience, in addition to the overall conflict of the novel. Think about the section you just read and identify at least five conflicts. They can be conflicts that characters are experiencing throughout the entire book or ones they encountered during your selected reading.

When your group meets, write how the character(s) solved the problem. If the problem has not been solved, predict your own resolutions based on what you know about the characters.

Problem	Solution (Actual or Predicted)

Read-Aloud Master

Name_____

Book _____

Select six passages from the text that are important or interesting. Mark these passages with a sticky note and write the page/paragraph on the lines below. After you choose your passages, you must explain the author's purpose for each passage. In other words, what message was the author trying to get across or why was that part included?

When your group meets, you may read the passages aloud to the group, or ask another person to read the selection. After your group reads each one, discuss why the author included that part in the story. Allow your group members to share their thoughts first. Then share what you wrote.

Page/Paragraph	Significance of Passage
1. _____	_____
	_____
	_____
	_____
	_____
2. _____	_____
	_____
	_____
	_____
	_____
3. _____	_____
	_____
	_____
	_____
	_____

Read-Aloud Master *(cont.)*

Page/Paragraph **Significance of Passage**

4. _____ _____

_____

_____

_____

_____

5. _____ _____

_____

_____

_____

_____

6. _____ _____

_____

_____

_____

_____

Adapted from Daniels, H. *Literature Circles: Voice and Choice in the Student-Centered Classroom.*
York, ME: Stenhouse Publishers, 1994.

Scene Setter

Name_____

Book _____

When reading a book, it is important to know the setting (where things are happening). Sometimes the settings can change. Trace where things happen each reading. Write the name of the place, page in the book, and then describe the place with detail. You may map or chart the each scene on the back of this page.

Action begins:

_____   _____   _____
       Location   Page   _____

                                              _____

Key places/actions during reading:

_____   _____   _____
       Location   Page

_____   _____   _____
       Location   Page

_____   _____   _____
       Location   Page

Action ends:

_____   _____   _____
       Location   Page

Adapted from Daniels, H. *Literature Circles: Voice and Choice in the Student-Centered Classroom.* Stenhouse Publishers, 1994.

Sensational Sequels

Name _____

Book _____

Write a sequel (Part 2) for the book you have just finished. Complete the form below. On another sheet of paper, write an explanation of what will happen in your book or prepare to share a written excerpt from your new book with the class.

Title of the book you read: _____

Author: _____

Title of your sequel: _____

Setting of your book: _____

Is this the same as Part 1?   Yes   No   Explain: _____

_____

Protagonist (main character) of your book: _____

Description of the protagonist: _____

Is this the same protagonist as Part 1?   Yes   No   Explain: _____

_____

Antagonist (opponent) of your book: _____

Description of the antagonist: _____

Is this the same antagonist as Part 1?   Yes   No   Explain: _____

_____

What are some things that are the same in each book? _____

_____

_____

What are some things that are different in each book? _____

_____

_____

64

Sequencer

Name_____

Book _____

Write eight sentences that include the important events that occurred during the reading. Each sentence should be a different event. For each event, be sure you have included the answers to the following questions: Who? (character names), Did What? (the event), When?, and Where? (the setting). Cut the sentences apart on the dashed lines and have your group sequence the events.

As a group, decide which sentence tells the most important thing that happened in your reading and place a star next to it. Be careful not to use words like *first, then,* or *next.* When you turn these in, staple the events in order with your name on top.

Summarizer

Name_____

Book _____

Write a brief summary of the reading—beginning, middle, and end. Be sure you have included the answers to the following questions: Who? (character names), Did What? (the events), When?, and Where? (the settings).

When your group meets, share your summary. Then, on the next page, write a one-sentence summary of your reading. Your sentence should include the answers to the following questions: Who? (character names), Did What? (the event), When?, and Where? (the setting).

Beginning:_____

_____

_____

_____

_____

_____

_____

Middle: _____

_____

_____

_____

_____

_____

_____

_____

Summarizer (cont.)

End: _____

_____

_____

_____

_____

_____

_____

_____

_____

_____

Group Summary (1–2 sentences): _____

_____

_____

_____

_____

Adapted from Daniels, H. *Literature Circles: Voice and Choice in the Student-Centered Classroom.* Stenhouse Publishers, 1994.

Timeliner

Name _____

Book _____

Timeliner is another way to show events over a period of time. Your job is to create a time line for your reading. The time line may show events over a period of one day, a week, month, year, or many years. If specific times or dates are unknown, discuss this with your group and come to an agreement on a time period or time frame. Collect the data and represent it on a time line that has been created with paper and pencil or on the computer. Use the following guidelines when creating your time line:

- With your group, discuss the time period in which the events take place.

- Decide what increments of time (hours, days, weeks, years, etc.) you will use.

- Select five or more significant events from your reading.

- You may include pictures to enhance your time line.

- Your time line may be merged with other time lines from this book, a different book, or another subject as a final project.

On this paper, brainstorm the time element and the events from your assignment. Attach a copy of your time line with this paper to be turned in to the teacher.

Chapter	When (time element)	Event

Trait Tracker

Name_____

Book _____

Character maps can show us a character's traits and how he or she acts toward others based on the settings or events in the story. Think of a character in the selection you just read. Write the name in the main circle. What are four traits that describe this character? Write them in the diamond shapes. Think of evidence from the story to support the trait listed for the character. Write the evidence in the rectangles. When your group meets, read the traits and have them try to guess the character. Do they agree or disagree with your ideas?

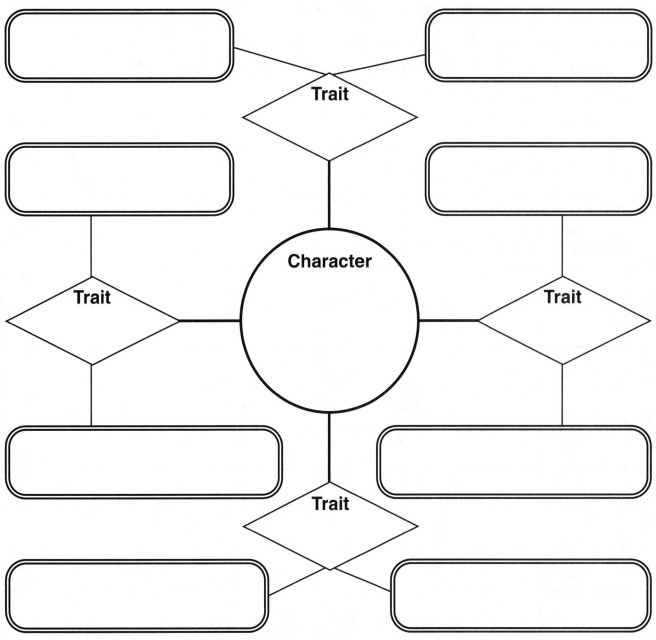

"Wanted!" Poster

Name _____

Book _____

Is there a character in the story you just read who is bad? Is there one who is really good? Create a "Wanted!" poster for a character in the story. Decide why he or she is wanted, list identifying traits, where he or she was last seen, and what the reward would be for his or her capture. Complete the poster with an illustration of the character.

WANTED!

Wanted for: _____

Gender: _____ Height: _____ Weight: _____

Eye Color: _____ Hair Color: _____ Skin Color: _____

Identifying Features: _____

_____

Last seen: _____

Reward: _____

Word Webs

Name _____

Book _____

Select four words from your assignment. Write one word in the center of each web. Decide on four attributes you will use to identify the word, and write them on the spokes of the web (*These may include the following: Looks Like, Sounds Like, Smells Like, Tastes Like, Feels Like, Usual Uses, Unusual Uses, Synonyms, Antonyms*). Then, add words that fit the attribute category and describe the word in the center of the web.

A sample is done for you.

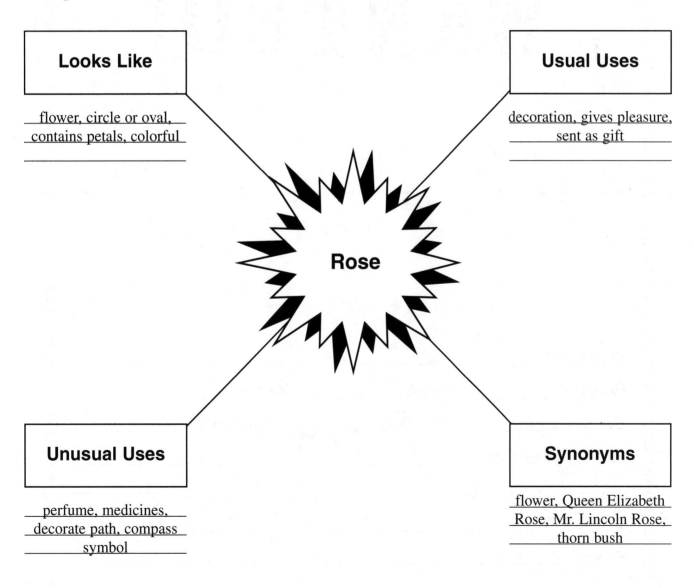

Looks Like

flower, circle or oval, contains petals, colorful

Usual Uses

decoration, gives pleasure, sent as gift

Rose

Unusual Uses

perfume, medicines, decorate path, compass symbol

Synonyms

flower, Queen Elizabeth Rose, Mr. Lincoln Rose, thorn bush

Word Webs *(cont.)*

Word Webs (cont.)

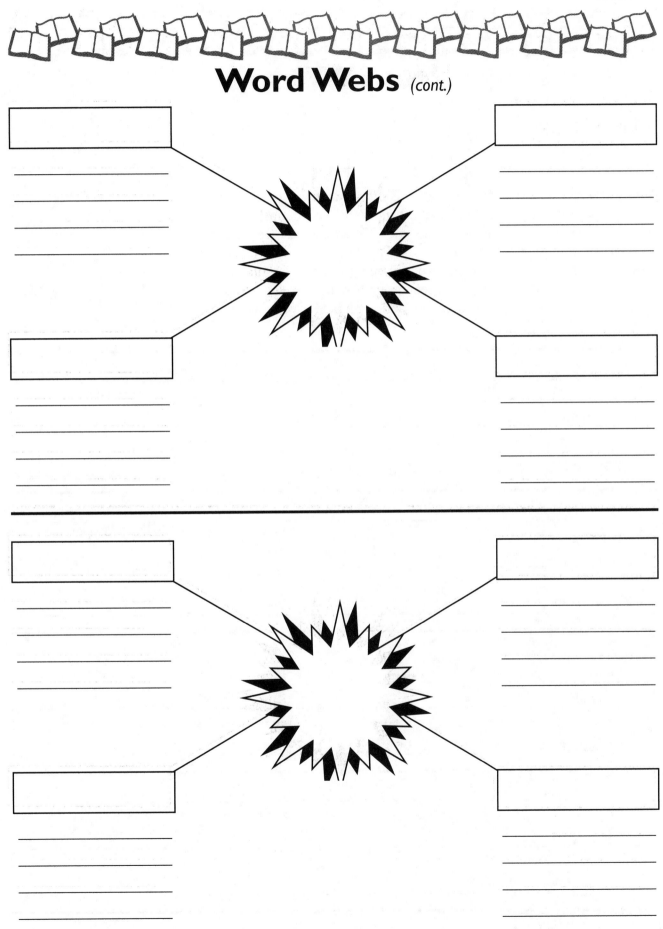

Word Wizard

Name_____

Book _____

Your job is to pick out eight new or confusing words from your reading. You are to look them up in the dictionary and write their definition according to the use of the word in the story. Be sure to include the page number and paragraph number where you found the word. Then create a new sentence using the vocabulary word correctly. When your group meets, share each word and read aloud the sentence where the word is found in the book. Have your group try to guess the definition before you read it to them.

1. _____ _____ _____
   (word)   *(page)*   *(paragraph)*

   Definition: _____

   Sentence: _____

2. _____ _____ _____
   (word)   *(page)*   *(paragraph)*

   Definition: _____

   Sentence: _____

3. _____ _____ _____
   (word)   *(page)*   *(paragraph)*

   Definition: _____

   Sentence: _____

4. _____ _____ _____
   (word)   *(page)*   *(paragraph)*

   Definition: _____

   Sentence: _____

74

Word Wizard (cont.)

5. _____   _____   _____
   (word)   (page)   (paragraph)

   Definition: _____

   Sentence: _____

6. _____   _____   _____
   (word)   (page)   (paragraph)

   Definition: _____

   Sentence: _____

7. _____   _____   _____
   (word)   (page)   (paragraph)

   Definition: _____

   Sentence: _____

8. _____   _____   _____
   (word)   (page)   (paragraph)

   Definition: _____

   Sentence: _____

Role Review

Place the Role Review sheets (pages 76–78) in your journal or literature folder. Use them as a reference for completing each role.

Action Plot-O-Graph

Rate the intensity of the action and chart it on a bar graph.

Advice Columnist

Write a letter from a character who has conflict in the story. Then write a response to that character giving him or her advice on how to deal with the conflict.

A Sense of Character

Put yourself in the position of the character and decide how he or she may be using his or her senses.

A Time of Change

Reflect on the experiences a character in the story has had and how he or she has changed because of these events.

Character Connections

Show how you connect with a character based on similar likes, dislikes, or interests.

Character Profile

Based on clues and evidence in the story, complete a profile about the character.

Character Web

Use a web to show how characters are related, and site evidence from the text to support your findings.

Circle Sequencer

Show the main event of a story and the actions that led up to that event.

Commentator

Facts can be proven, but opinions cannot. Give examples of statements in the text that are facts and opinions.

Connection Maker

Show connections between the text you are reading and the same text, other text, the world, and yourself.

Discussion Leader

Create various levels of questions to guide your group in a discussion of the passage.

Dream Weaver

Draw a picture of what one of the characters might dream about and why that is significant to them. Cite examples from the text.

Role Review *(cont.)*

Efficient Effector

Show cause-and-effect relationships between events in the story.

Emotional Events

Describe events in the story that elicited certain emotions in you or a character.

Fortune Teller

Make predictions about what might happen next in the story, based on evidence from the text.

Illustrator

Draw a picture that depicts an important character, event, setting, or problem. Explain the significance of the picture.

Map Matters

Draw a map and label where significant events took place.

Meaningful Mottos

Create a motto that a character would live by, based on evidence in the reading.

Meeting of the Minds

Investigate two opposing characters' points of view on an issue or conflict in the story.

Memory Maker

Create a scrapbook that a character might keep depicting at least five areas of importance to that character.

New Narrator

Choose a minor character in the story and tell the story from his or her point of view.

News Reporter

Write a news article answering *who, what, where, when,* and *why* about an event in your reading.

Perfect Puzzler

Create a vocabulary word puzzle on paper, or use a computer program if one is available.

Poetic Perceptions

Write a poem about a character in the story. Use the format given or one recently studied in class.

Point/Counterpoint

Explain how you disagree with a character's thoughts or actions and what you would have done differently. Tell how your actions would have changed the path of the story.

Role Review (cont.)

Power Graph

Select two characters and plot their power (intensity, prominence, or influence) throughout the story.

Problem Solver

Identify conflicts in the story and show how they were solved.

Read-Aloud Master

Identify and explain the significance of six interesting sections of the text to share with your group.

Scene Setter

Track the action from the reading. Describe the setting and action in detail with words or an action map.

Sensational Sequels

Use the guided questions to write a sequel to the story.

Sequencer

Write eight events that occurred in the reading, cut them apart, and have your group put them back in order. Decide which event was the most important for that section of the story.

Summarizer

Write a brief summary of the reading. Be sure to include the answers to the following questions: *who, did what, when,* and *where.*

Timeliner

Create a time line of events on paper or on a computer program if one is available. Have the group decide on time increments, and try to merge the time line with others from history or other parts of the book.

Trait Tracker

List a character's traits and find evidence from the text that supports your finding.

"Wanted!" Poster

Create a "Wanted!" poster for a character in the story. Explain why he or she is wanted, list identifying traits, where he or she was last seen, and what reward is being offered.

Word Webs

List four attributes to help identify four words selected from the text.

Word Wizard

Look up eight new or confusing words in the dictionary, write the definition of each according to its use in the passage, and create an original sentence using the word.

What extensions complement literature circles?

79

Sharing Showcase: Teacher List

When a literature circle has finished a book, the group may share their reading with the class through a presentation that celebrates and culminates what they have learned. Groups may choose one of the activities below or have a different idea approved by the teacher. It is helpful to provide each student with a list of the options to keep in their folder for reference throughout the year. Below is an explanation of Sharing Showcase activities. Following this section is a list that can be copied and distributed to the class (page 83).

Reminders

✓ All group members will participate in the presentation.

✓ All group members will receive the same grade.

✓ A presentation should last around 5–10 minutes.

✓ No more than two class periods should be spent preparing for the presentation.

Sharing Showcase Activities

- **Museum display of artifacts from the book**

  Each member of the group brings in or creates an artifact that represents a character, setting, or event in the book. A brief explanation of the artifact and its significance to the story should be written. The artifacts are then put on display for the class to view.

- **Scrapbook of the book**

  Just as students keep a scrapbook of vacations or activities, they can make a scrapbook of the book. The scrapbook could focus on one or all of the characters, the setting, events, or overall plot or theme. Scrapbook contents should have labels to explain what they are and their significance.

- **Large story map of the book**

  A poster-size map of the story can show where the action takes place. The story may have taken place in a building, a small town, a city, a certain country, or on an entire continent. The map should show the direction of the action and have a key for identifying features.

- **Poetry connecting themes in the book**

  A book of poetry can be original work combined with works by others that relate to the theme. It may also be an original piece about the entire book. If poetry is being studied in class, the teacher may want to require a certain type of poem or pieces from several different formats. A brief explanation should accompany the poem, stating how the pieces connect.

Sharing Showcase: Teacher List *(cont.)*

- **Poster advertising a movie based on the book**

  Students should use newspapers and magazines to cut out pictures of well-known people to play the part in a movie about the book. The poster should tell the roles that the person is playing as well as audience-grabbing information to entice viewers.

- **Reader's Theater**

  Reader's Theater differs from a play in that the acting is done only with the voice. There are no sound effects, props, or scenery. As a group the students determine which part of the book they would like to perform. A script is written specifying everyone's lines. Students perform the reading in front of the class.

- **A sequel to the story or a new ending for the book**

  A sequel to the story could be just another added chapter. As a group, the students can determine what might happen next. They should give their chapter a title, describe the setting, identify the main character (protagonist), and the character that is causing the conflict (antagonist) if appropriate. The sequel should flow from the main book and make sense with the actions and plot presented by the original author.

- **A time line of the story**

  A time line shows how the events in the story happened over time. As a group, this can be done on a large sheet of paper or poster board. It can also be done on the computer (See the Software list on page 122.). The time line should include the span of time, the major events of the story, and illustrations if desired.

- **Report on the author's life**

  Students can investigate various encyclopedias and online sources to find information on the author of the book they just read. The report may include other works by the same author, description of the author's writing style, personal background, and education.

- **Collages representing different characters**

  This is similar to the Character Mapping role but on a grand scale. Students can use various media for creating the collage (magazine, newspapers, personal drawings, etc.).

- **An original skit based on the book**

  Unlike Reader's Theater, the group can not only write a script for a significant part of the book but they would also perform it in front of the class with minor props and scenery.

- **A new cover for the book**

  Individually or as a group, the students can create a new cover for the book. The cover could be based on a particular character, the conflict, or a particular event in the story.

Sharing Showcase: Teacher List (cont.)

- **An advertising campaign for the book**

  The goal for the group is to entice other students to want to read the book. The advertising campaign can be done on video as a commercial, on the computer, on posters, or any combination of media.

- **Diary of a character**

  A diary can be a very personal look into a person, or, in this case, a character. It should offer insight to the character's state of mind and personal views that may have been implied in the story. The diary can be several entries pertaining to one event or several entries on the same event that show how the character has changed over the course of action.

- **Interview with a character**

  An interview with a character requires good insightful questions to be planned. Information from Bloom's Taxonomy can be shared with students to guide them in creating higher-level questions. The questions should offer a personal view of a character, not merely recount an event in the book.

- **A song or dance about the book**

  Some students relate better through music and movement. This can be a great opportunity for them to share their talent while also sharing what they know or learned about the book.

- **News broadcast of events from the book**

  Like Reader's Theater and performing a skit, this activity requires the students to write a script and perform in front of the class. Prior to creating a news broadcast, it may be helpful to identify what makes an effective broadcast by critiquing the news on local stations.

- **Letter recommending the book for purchase in the library**

  What better way to promote reading than to petition the school or local library to stock up on copies of that book? Why not even start a campaign to raise money to purchase the book for the class library?

- **Impersonation of key characters**

  With props and costumes, students can impersonate the characters from their book for the class period or even for the entire day. To impersonate for the entire day would certainly get them talking about the book and possibly lead others to read it.

- **Background/research on the setting or time period**

  This activity can be paired with the time line activity to show how events in the book relate to historical events.

Sharing Showcase: Student List

When your literature circle has finished the book, you need to share your reading with the class through a 5–10 minute presentation that celebrates and culminates what you have learned. You may choose one of the activities below or have a different idea approved by the teacher. Sharing Showcase presentations will be graded on cooperation, content, presentation, and visual aides that are used.

- Museum display of artifacts from the book

- Scrapbook of the book

- Large story map of the book

- Poetry connecting themes in the book

- Poster advertising a movie based on the book

- Reader's Theater

- A sequel to the story or a new ending for the book

- A time line of the story

- Report on the author's life

- Collages representing different characters

- An original skit based on the book

- A new cover for the book

- An advertising campaign for the book

- Diary of a character

- Interview with a character

- A song or dance about the book

- News broadcast of events from the book

- Letter recommending the book for purchase in the library

- Impersonation of key characters

- Background/research on the setting or time period

The content of each presentation must include the following:	
• **Title**	• **Plot**
• **Setting**	• **Conflict**
• **Characters**	• **Book Review**
• **Theme**	

Assessment of Sharing Showcases

Sharing showcases are culminating activities that allow students to express what they have learned in a way that is meaningful to them. Sharing showcases should not be the only source of grading for the book unit. In order for a group to do a Sharing Showcase, all members of that group must participate. They will be graded as a group and all students of that group will receive the same grade for the Sharing Showcase activity. Students should use no more than two class periods planning their showcase before presenting it to the class or teacher. If a presentation is involved, it should be no longer than five to 10 minutes long. On the next pages are a sample rubric that can be used for assessing a Sharing Showcase project and an evaluation form.

Sharing Showcase Rubric

Group _____ Book _____

Score _____ (12 points total)	1 Point	2 Points	3 Points
Cooperation	Your group experienced many difficulties along the way. Teacher intervention was necessary.	Your group experienced some difficulty. You were able to resolve them with little teacher intervention.	Your group knows the meaning of teamwork.
Content	Your group was missing three or more key components.	Your group had one or more missing or incomplete components.	Your group was able to integrate all key components.
Presentation	It was obvious that your group was not prepared to present.	Your presentation did not flow smoothly! More practice would have been helpful.	It was evident that your group was prepared to present.
Visual Aids	Visuals were poorly constructed or not used at all.	More effort would have enhanced your visual aids.	Visuals were well done.

Sharing Showcase Evaluation Form

Group _____ Date _____

Activity _____ Book _____

The group will be scored on the following components of the group's Sharing Showcase activity. Each member of the group will receive the same grade since it was a group effort.

Showcase Component	Score
Characters (development) Comments:	_____
Setting (time and place) Comments:	_____
Theme (examples for support) Comments:	_____
Plot (important events) Comments:	_____
Conflict (problems and solutions) Comments:	_____
Book Review (analysis of elements) Comments:	_____
Quality of Work Comments:	_____
Group Work (cooperation) Comments:	_____
Presentation (organized) Comments:	_____
	_____/50 Total

Book Lover's Journal

Depending on your resources and the organization of your classroom, you can choose to organize your journals or notebooks in a variety of ways. Each student should have their own journal and a safe place to keep it in the classroom.

One way is to use spiral notebooks with at least 75 pages. Use the inside front cover as a table of contents and have students number the pages so they can mark the beginning of each section. One useful method is to fold a sticky label with the name of the section on it over the edge of the paper to mark the beginning of a section. Students can then quickly find the section they need. A second way to organize journals is to use a three-ring binder. Students can use dividers with tabs to label their sections. Notebook paper can be inserted as needed.

The following are suggested sections to include in a Book Lover's Journal.

Books I've Read

Students keep a running record of the books they have read. Genres and authors' names are recorded so patterns can be seen in their reading choices and appropriate books can be recommended. Literature circle books, independent books, and teacher read-aloud sessions can all be recorded. See page 91 for an example.

For assessment, depending on expectations for the number of books read, award points for each book read. For example, the requirement could be four books per quarter with each worth two points. Students that go beyond the expectation can be awarded extra points. Points can also be subtracted for incomplete forms.

Book Lover's Journal *(cont.)*

Books I Want to Read

When kids vote on books they want to read in literature circles, have them record their choices here, so they can go back and read the books independently if they are not chosen for that group. When students share books they are reading, such as in the fish bowl situation (page 105), students can record books that catch their attention. When they are looking for books to read, this is the section they can turn to! See pages 92 and 93 for examples.

For assessment, students are expected to add three or more books or topics to their list per theme. This is easily attained since students should be completing them during the voting process at the beginning of a new literature circle group.

Mini-Lessons

Mini-lessons are explicit skill lessons used to teach students the reading strategies that will apply on the literature circle role sheets. When new strategies or skills are taught, students can record definitions, examples, etc. in this section of their journal. This becomes useful for students to refer to throughout the year. To become more familiar with teaching mini-lessons in reading, refer to Cris Tovani and Ellin Keene's book *I Read It, but I Don't Get It; Strategies That Work* by Stephanie Harvey and Anne Goudirs; or *Mosaic of Thought* by Ellin Keene and Susan Zimmermann. See pages 94–101 for examples of mini-lesson topics, related picture book titles, and corresponding roles.

For assessment, notebooks are checked for notes taken during mini-lessons. Students who are absent are expected to copy the notes from the teacher or a peer. If the notes are complete, four points are awarded for each entry. If items are missing, no points are given. This is an easy way for students to gain points and to build responsibility for missed work while showing the importance of the mini-lesson content.

Teacher Conferences

Depending on the format used for student conferences, teachers can use this section to record student responses, keep running records on oral reading, list suggestions for the student to work on, etc. This becomes a useful resource for parent-teacher conferences because it can be used to show growth throughout the year. See page 109 for an explanation of conferences and page 110 for a sample conference form.

88

Book Lover's Journal (cont.)

Reader Response

This section can be used in a variety of ways. Teachers can give students prompts depending on the books they are reading, or teachers can brainstorm a list with the students for them to choose. See the section on dialogue journals for the process on brainstorming and suggestions for Reader Response prompts. This section can also be used when utilizing the double entry diary approach, or T-charts. For assessment, see page 102.

Dialogue Entry

Dialogue entries are reciprocal responses to student-generated prompts. After students read, they write back and forth to one another discussing their reactions to their literature circle book. The most common procedure would be for two students to alternate writing in their shared journal for the duration of the book. However for students to be exposed to a variety of interpretations it is suggested to provide each student with his or her own journal, allow students to input personal responses to a prompt of his or her choice, and pass the journal to a group member on their right or left. Each student will read the previous entry and write a reaction and possibly raise new issues. Students enjoy passing "notes" back and forth!

Variations for the dialogue entry are as follows:

- Journals could be passed around the entire group to get numerous responses to a single prompt as done with Round Table Discussions (page 106).
- Do book buddy journals over e-mail with another class in or outside the school or district.
- Post a book review on the Internet at *amazon.com* or other book review sites.
- Do a traditional book buddy journal with another grade level with the same or a different book.

Brainstorm with the class a list of prompts and topic suggestions for journal entries prior to implementing dialogue entries, or have students use the list on the next page as a guide. For assessment, see page 102.

Student Prompts and Topic Suggestions

Prompts

I think . . . _____

I hope . . . _____

I believe . . . _____

I can't believe . . . _____

I imagine . . . _____

In my opinion . . . _____

This reminds me of . . . _____

I wonder . . . _____

I agree/disagree . . . _____

I predict . . . _____

I would like to know about . . . _____

I wonder why . . . _____

I don't understand . . . _____

This section made me think of . . . _____

Topics

Characters: _____

Plot: _____

Conflicts: _____

Setting: _____

Resolution: _____

Opinions: _____

Connections: _____

Feelings: _____

Favorite/Scariest/Funniest part: _____

Author's style of writing: _____

Comparison to other books, stories, movies: _____

Question about confusing parts: _____

Summarize or retell the reading: _____

Imagery formed by descriptive language: _____

Books I've Read

Name _____

Date Started	Date Ended	Title and Author	Genre	Rating

Books I Want to Read

Name _____

Title	Author	Genre	Who recommended the book to me?

Books I Want to Read (cont.)

Books I Want to Read	Favorite Authors

Reading Mini-Lessons

Mini-Lesson	Skills	Picture Books	Literature Circle Roles
What do good readers do before, during, and after reading?	• Developing a purpose • Previewing text • Building background knowledge • Monitoring understanding of text using comprehension strategies	• *Dog Breath: The Horrible Trouble with Hally Tosis* by Dav Pilkey • *Tops and Bottoms* by Janet Stevens • *The Wednesday Surprise* by Eve Bunting • *The Matzah that Papa Brought Home* by Fran Manushkin • *The Story of Ruby Bridges* by Robert Coles	All role sheets that focus on reading strategies are included in the following mini-lessons: • Visualizing • Previewing and Predicting • Questioning • Connections • Background Knowledge • Inferring • Determining Importance
Coding Text	• Using codes to aid students in monitoring their meaning • Identifying fiction/nonfiction	• *Baseball Saved Us* by Ken Mochizuki • *Some Birthday* by Patricia Pollacco • *Chester's Way* by Kevin Henkes • *Amber on the Mountain* by Tony Johnston • *Aunt Chip and the Great Triple Creek Dam Affair* by Patricia Polacco	• Fortune Teller • Connection Maker • Illustrator • Read-Aloud Master
Visualizing	• Monitoring meaning • Creating pictures in the mind to enhance comprehension	• *Twilight Comes Twice* by Ralph Fletcher • *Seven Blind Mice* by Ed Young • *Appalachia* by Cynthia Rylant • *Night in the Country* by Cynthia Rylant • *A Drop of Water* by Walter Wick • *Fireflies* by Julie Brinckloe • *Owl Moon* by Jane Yolen • *All I See* by Cynthia Rylant • *The Art Lesson* by Tomie de Paola	• Character Profile • Dream Weaver • Illustrator • Map Matters • Memory Maker • Scene Setter

Reading Mini-Lessons (cont.)

Mini-Lesson	Skills	Picture Books	Literature Circle Roles
Questioning	• Self-questioning • I Wonder . . . • Levels of Questioning • Bloom's Taxonomy (pages 10–12)	• *Charlie Anderson* by Barbara Abercrombie • *How Come?* by Kathy Wollard • *The Day of Ahmed's Secret* by Florence Parry Heide • *Big Al* by Andrew Clements • *The Garden of Abdul Gasazi* by Chris Van Allsburg • *The Sweetest Fig* by Chris Van Allsburg • *The Widow's Broom* by Chris Van Allsburg • *Math Curse* by Jon Scieszka	• Discussion Leader • Point/Counterpoint
Connections	• Connecting the text to world issues and events, to the personal life of the reader, to other texts, and to other parts within the text • Responding to the text using personal experiences and feelings	• *My Rotten Redheaded Brother* by Cynthia Rylant • *The Wall* by Eve Bunting • *The Relatives Came* by Patricia Polacco • *Welcome to the Ice House* by Jan Yolen • *Tough Cookie* by David Wisniewski • *Thank You, Mr. Falker* by Patricia Polacco • *The Tenth Good Thing About Barney* by Judith Viorst	• A Sense of Character • Character Connections • Character Profile • Discussion Leader • Emotional Events
Book Lover's Journal	• Organizing journals • Setting expectations • See pages 87–89.	• *Amelia's Notebook* by Marissa Moss • *Rachel's Journal: The Story of a Pioneer Girl* by Marissa Moss • *The Gardner* by Sarah Stewart	Not applicable
Team Building	• "Getting to know you" activities • Setting class expectations for group work • Developing respect	• *The Raft* by Jim LaMarche • *Roxaboxen* by Alice McLerrn • *The Crayon Box that Talked* by Shane DeRolf • *Crickwing* by Janell Cannon	All role sheets encourage teamwork when students share.

Reading Mini-Lessons (cont.)

Mini-Lesson	Skills	Picture Books	Literature Circle Roles
Reader's Voices	• Listening to the voices in our heads to have a conversation with the text	• *A Gathering of Flowers: Stories About Being Young in America* by Joyce Carol Thomas • *What Do Fish Have to Do with Anything? And Other Stories* by Avi • *Throwing Shadows* by E.L. Konigsburg • *Every Living Thing* by Cynthia Rylant • *Baseball in April and Other Stories* by Gary Soto • *Twelve Impossible Things Before Breakfast Stories* by Jane Yolen	All role sheets that focus on reading strategies are included in the following mini-lessons: • Visualizing • Previewing and Predicting • Questioning • Connections • Background Knowledge • Inferring • Determining Importance
Background Knowledge	• Using background knowledge to make meaning of the text • Creating background knowledge • Correcting inaccurate background knowledge	• *Fish is Fish* by Leo Loini • *Hurricane* by David Wiesner • *Ira Sleeps Over* by Bernard Wader • *Baseball Saved Us* by Ken Mochizuki • *Pink and Say* by Patricia Polacco • *B is for Buckeye* by Marcia Schonberg • *A Day's Work* by Eve Bunting • *Going Home* by Eve Bunting	• Discussion Leader • Dream Weaver • Illustrator
Previewing and Predicting	• Using background knowledge and textual evidence to make predictions • Previewing the text to create background knowledge • Use textual features to make predictions	• *The Sweetest Fig* by Chris Van Allsburg • *Old Jake's Skirts* by C. Anne Scott • *Reuben and the Blizzard* by Merle Good • *The Wednesday Surprise* by Eve Bunting • *Grandpa's Teeth* by Rod Clement • *The Pain and the Great One* by Judy Blume	• Advice Columnist • Discussion Leader • Dream Weaver • Fortune Teller • Point/Counterpoint • Problem Solver • Sensational Sequels

Reading Mini-Lessons (cont.)

Mini-Lesson	Skills	Picture Books	Literature Circle Roles
Determining Importance	• Main idea vs. detail • Retelling • Summary	• *The True Story of the 3 Little Pigs* by Jon Scieszka • *The 3 Little Wolves and the Big Bad Pig* by Eugene Trivizas • *They Walk the Earth* by Seymour Simon • *An Island Scrapbook: Dawn to Dusk on a Barrier Island* by Virginia Wright-Frierson • *Keiko's Story: The Real Life Tale of the World's Most Famous Killer Whale* by Diane Coplin Hammond • *Dinosaurs* by Gail Gibbons • *Seashore Babies* by Kathy Darling	• New Narrator • Point/Counterpoint • Timeliner • Circle Sequencer • Discussion Leader • Scene Setter • Efficient Effector • Map Matters • Memory Maker • News Reporter • Sequencer • Summarizer • Timeliner
Story Elements	• Point of View • Theme • Characters • Setting • Plot	• *Lily's Purple Plastic Purse* by Kevin Henkes • *As the Crow Flies* by Gail Hartman • *Best Friends* by Steven Kellog • *Miss Rumphius* by Barbara Cooney • *Two Bad Ants* by Chris Van Allsburg • *Voices in the Park* by Anthony Browne • *Squids Will Be Squids* by Jon Scieszka	• Trait Tracker • Timeliner • Scene Setter • News Reporter • New Narrator • Meaningful Mottos • Meeting of the Minds • Map Matters • Summarizer • Point/Counterpoint • Advice Columnist • A Sense of Character • A Time of Change • Character Connections • Character Web • Circle Sequencer • Emotional Events • Sequencer • Poetic Perceptions • Illustrator • "Wanted!" Poster

Reading Mini-Lessons *(cont.)*

Mini-Lesson	Skills	Picture Books	Literature Circle Roles
Compare/Contrast	• Identify similarities and differences among story elements including characters, settings, conflicts, etc.	• *Pink and Say* by Patricia Polacco • *I Didn't Know that Crocodiles Yawn* by Kate Petty • *Grandfather's Journey* by Allen Say • *Bugs and Other Insects* by Bobbie Kalman and Tammy Everts • *Rosie and Michael* by Judith Viorst	• Character Connections • Discussion Leader • Emotional Events • Meeting of the Minds • Point/Counterpoint • Timeliner
Problem/Solution	• Internal vs. external conflicts • Making smart choices • Discussion Web • Point of View	• *The War Between the Vowels and the Consonants* by Priscilla Turner • *The Wump World* by Bill Peet • *Piggie Pie* by Margie Palatini • *And the Dish Ran Away with the Spoon* by Janet Stevens • *Click! Clack! Moo!: Cows That Type* by Doreen Cronin • *The Pain and the Great One* by Judy Blume	• Advice Columnist • Discussion Leader • Meeting of the Minds • Point/Counterpoint • Problem Solver • "Wanted!" Poster • Summarizer
Cause/Effect	• Linking words • Using "because" to determine relationship • Implied relationships • Making predictions about the effects of a cause	• *Where Once There Was a Wood* by Denise Fleming • *It Wasn't My Fault* by Helen Lester • *The Most Beautiful Roof in the World* by Kathryn Lasky • *The Bracelet* by Yoshiko Uchida • *Alexander Who Use to Be Rich Last Sunday* by Judith Viorst • *If You Give a Pig a Pancake* by Laura Numeroff • *Mistakes that Worked* by Charlotte Foltz Jones	• Advice Columnist • Circle Sequencer • Discussion Leader • Efficient Effector • Point/Counterpoint
Fact/Opinion	• Facts can be proven either true or false. Everyone will come to the same conclusion. • Statements of opinion say "take my word for it" • Key words for opinion statements	• *Ghosts of the White House* by Cheryl Harness • *So You Want to Be President?* by David Small • *Rachel's Journal: The Story of a Pioneer Girl* by Marissa Moss • *Lives of the Presidents: Fame, Shame, and What the Neighbors Thought* by Kathleen Krull • *Snowflake Bentley* by Jacqueline Briggs Martin • *Chameleons Are Cool* by Martin Jenkins	• Commentator • Advice Columnist • Discussion Leader • Meeting of the Minds • News Reporter • Point/Counterpoint • "Wanted!" Poster

98

Reading Mini-Lessons *(cont.)*

Mini-Lesson	Skills	Picture Books	Literature Circle Roles
Author's Influence	• Tone—either positive, negative, or neutral • Attitude—either approval or disapproval • Purpose—to inform, to persuade, to entertain • Identify differences in fiction/nonfiction	• *Wolf Watch* by Kay Winters • *Voices of the Alamo* by Sherry Garland • *Roxaboxen* by Alice McLerran • *Faithful Elephants: A True Story of Animals, People, and War* by Yukio Tsuchya • *Terrible Things* by Even Bunting • *Amelia's Road* by Linda Jacobs Altman • *Dear Willie Rudd* by Libba Moore Gray	• Discussion Leader • Meaningful Mottos • Read-Aloud Master • Poetic Perceptions
Reader's Purpose	• The reason for reading the text • Determines what is important in the text and what is remembered • Use strategies to choose independent reading for their own purposes	Teachers select the book to model a purpose for reading (reading for information, reading for pleasure). Students select independent books to share depending on their purposes.	All roles create a purpose for the reader —that is one of the benefits!
Book Review	• Express reasons for recommending or not recommending the text • Evaluate story elements	Any of the picture books listed	• Discussion Leader See roles in Story Elements mini-lesson.
Fix-Up Strategies	• Repairing meaning using reading strategies • Using word structure and context cues	Short text according to instructional reading level Poetry—See selected texts in poetry mini-lesson.	• Perfect Puzzler • Word Wizard • Word Webs

Reading Mini-Lessons *(cont.)*

Mini-Lesson	Skills	Picture Books	Literature Circle Roles
Poetry	• Literary devices including alliteration, simile, metaphor, personification, etc. • Author's Influence • Interpreting • Connecting with texts	• *Brown Angels* by Walter Dean Myers • *No More Homework! No More Tests!* by Bruce Lanksy • *Beneath a Blue Umbrella* by Jack Prelutsky • *Dirty Laundry Pile: Poems in Different Voices* by Paul B. Janeczko • *I Am Phoenix: Poems for Two Voices* by Paul Fleischman • *Sometimes I Wonder if Poodles like Noodles* by Laura Numeroff • *Water Music* by Jane Yolen • *Poetry for Young People: Robert Frost* by Gary D. Schmidt • *Insectlopedia* by Douglas Florian	• Poetic Perception All role sheets can be used or modified depending on the poem
Oral Reading	• Fluency: reading in meaningful chunks • Self-monitoring: using fix-up strategies to correct miscues • Oral Expression: reading with a voice, follows the tone of the text	See mini-lesson on poetry for Poetry Books. • *Bugs* by Lynn Munsinger • *A Sip of Aesop* by Jane Yolen • *The Stinky Cheese Man and Other Fairly Stupid Tales* by Jon Scieska	• Read-Aloud Master • Poetic Perceptions
Genres	• Realistic Fiction • Historical Fiction • Fantasy • Traditional Literature • Informational Text • Biographies	All books listed fit in one of these categories.	• Discussion Leader

Reading Mini-Lessons *(cont.)*

Mini-Lesson	Skills	Picture Books	Literature Circle Roles
Inferring	• Reading between the lines • Text evidence + background knowledge = inference • Predicting, Questioning, Visualizing	• *Mysteries of Harris Burdick* by Chris Can Allsburg • *The Stranger* by Chris Van Allsburg • *The Wretched Stone* by Chris Van Allsburg • *Encounter* by Jane Yolen • *Dandelions* by Even Bunting • *Rose Blanche* by Roberto Innocenti • *The Mary Celeste: An Unsolved Mystery from History* by Jane Yolen • *History* by Jane Yolen	• Read-Aloud Master • Meaningful Mottos • A Sense of Character • A Time of Change • Character Profile • Discussion Leader • Dream Weaver • Fortune Teller • Illustrator • Memory Maker • Problem Solver • Sensational Sequels • New Narrator
Listening and Speaking Skills	• Active listening • Responding to the speaker • Asking relevant questions • Respecting the contributions of others	Book talks using short stories—See mini-lesson on Reader's Voices.	The sharing of all the role sheets encourages listening and speaking.
Sequencing	• Flashbacks • Element of time	• *The Gardner* by Sarah Stewart • *The Giving Tree* by Shel Silverstein • *A Busy Year* by Leo Leoni • *Salmon Summer* by Bruce McMillan • *Look to the North: Wolf Pup Diaries* by Jean Craighead George • *The True Story of the Three Little Pigs* by Jon Scieszka	• Circle Sequencer • Discussion Leader • Efficient Effector • Map Matters • Sensational Sequels • Sequencer • Scene Setter • Timeliner • Summarizer

Reader Response and Dialogue Entry Rubric

Group _____ Book _____

Score _____ (12 points total)	1 Point	2 Points	3 Points
Supporting Evidence from the Text	There is little or no evidence to support thoughts. More instruction and practice are needed.	Ideas are supported with adequate evidence from the text. Examples could have been expanded on or quotes included.	All ideas are fully supported with quotes or examples from the text.
Student Reaction to the Text	No reactions are evident or reactions given indicate that the student has not read the passage.	Reactions are given but their point of view is not clear and should be expanded upon.	The student's voice is heard through his or her opinions. Reactions to the text are plausible.
Displays an Understanding of the Text	Inaccurate or irrelevant details indicate a serious misunderstanding of the passage.	Evidence given is relevant and accurate but the student does not extend beyond the basic level of comprehension.	All evidence given is relevant and accurate. It is obvious the student is using all levels of comprehension skills.
Organization of Thoughts	The organization of this entry makes it difficult to assess the student.	Topics are scattered and not sequential. Thoughts and evidence do not always connect.	The entry flows in a manner that is easy for the reader to follow. Thoughts are followed by evidence.

Summer Reading Suggestions

Children need to be encouraged to continue their reading adventures through the summer. Providing them with a suggested book list, specific assignment, or incentives can help students make good choices for their summer reading. The following is a sample of an assignment that can be given to students in grades 5–8 and a sample of what is expected. Of course, this could be modified to meet the need of any grade or ability level.

Student Requirements for Summer Reading Book List

1. There should be a minimum of 15 books on the summer list.

   (Note: The minimum number of required books may be increased or decreased to meet the need of individual ability levels.)

2. The book list should be organized by genre first, and then alphabetized by author's last name.

   (Any format can be used for the student to organize their list. If genre is not being stressed, then the student can organize the list by author's name only. At the fourth-grade level, students should be encouraged to use proper bibliography format—author's last name, first name, and title of the book underlined).

3. Genres to be included on the list are below.

   (Include those that meet the needs of the curriculum and the students. Specify the number of books required from each genre.)

   - Realistic Fiction
   - Multicultural
   - Fantasy

   - Science Fiction
   - Autobiographies
   - Historical Fiction

   - Survival and Courage
   - Nonfiction
   - Biographies

4. Type a two-sentence description of the plot for each book. Use 12-point font. Include one sentence explaining why you chose to read the book.

   (The amount of written description can be modified to meet the needs of each student. Using a computer to type the description can be optional.)

5. Be creative!

Sample Summer Reading List

Realistic Fiction

Bauer, Joan. *Hope Was Here*

Hope was a 14-year-old girl who was hired to work as a waitress in a restaurant for 2½ years. Her mom abandoned her when she was a baby, so she lives and works with her Aunt Addie. Both of them take pride in their cooking. Joan Bauer is one of my favorite authors, and I wanted to read another one of her books.

Historical Fiction

Fleishman, Sid. *Bandit's Moon*

Annyrose was an orphan at age 12. She had left with a swindler during the Gold Rush. Even after dressing like a boy to escape, she was found by an outlaw named Joaquin Murieta. This book was recommended to me by my friend.

Fantasy

Avi. *Ragweed*

Ragweed is a rodent that hops on a train to the big city because he has his heart set on seeing the world. His new friends teach him about F.E.A.R. (Felines Enraged About Rodents) and their enemy President Silversides. I saw this book on the list and thought it would be interesting.

Nonfiction

Paulsen, Gary. *My Life in Dog Years*

Gary Paulsen is eager to share stories about the many dogs he has had throughout his life. He had Snowball as a young boy, Ike was his hunting buddy, and Josh was one of his border collies. He also had Electric Fred, Dirk the Grim Protector, and his best friend Pig. I have had several dogs and thought it would be interesting to read.

Fish Bowl

Literature circles work under the assumption that the students are capable of interacting or have been taught to interact in student-led discussion groups. The Fish Bowl is one activity to facilitate and model such group dynamics until the students are ready to lead the discussions on their own. The Fish Bowl also acts as a tool for students to share their enthusiasm and insights about their readings and inspire others to read the same book.

The Fish Bowl concept is based on the *Kiva*, the Hopi name for a sacred chamber. Traditionally, it is a large chamber built under or in the houses of a Pueblo village and is used as an assembly room for religious rites.

Directions

1. Set this up in the classroom using an inner circle and an outer circle of chairs.

2. Students that will be sharing their literature circle activities or tasks are seated in the inner circle with the Discussion Leader leading the group. The rest of the class is seated in the outer circle to listen and observe.

3. Initially, the teacher may want to lead the inner circle in the group discussion to model expectations. The teacher takes on the role of the Discussion Leader and leads the group through questions that were generated on the assignment.

4. Then, other group members are asked to share their assignments.

5. Questions and comments from the group are encouraged.

Outer Circle

Inner Circle

Variation

A vacant seat may be placed in the inner circle. If a student from the outer circle wishes to ask a question or make a comment, he or she is permitted to temporarily fill the vacant seat but must return to the outer circle once he or she has shared in order to afford others the same opportunity.

Round Table Discussions

Round table discussions are another way to get students to write about and talk about literature. The goal is to allow students the opportunity to discuss literature at their level. The objective is for students to participate in literary discussion groups by responding to higher-level comprehension questions, orally or in writing, regarding literature at their level.

Materials

- A chart with higher-level questions regarding the literature being studied. The number of questions should match the number of students in the group. (See sample questions from Bloom's Taxonomy on pages 10–12.)
- paper and pencil for each student
- timer

Directions

1. Divide students into literary groups. Students should be in groups of five. (This could be more or less depending on the needs of the students.)
2. Post the chart of comprehension questions so that all students can see it.
3. Make sure all students have paper and pencil.
4. Assign each member of the group a number (number 1, 2, etc.) depending on the number of students in the group. Have them write this number at the top of their paper. This is the number that will also correspond with the number to a question on the chart.
5. Review with the group each question and offer clarification if needed.
6. Each student will respond in writing to the question that corresponds to the number on his or her paper. Allow time for each student to review the question.
7. Start the timer allowing a predetermined amount of time for students to write their response (1–3 minutes). Ask students to put down their pencils when time is up.
8. Direct the students to fold their responses over to the back so that the next person cannot view it. They should then rewrite the number that corresponds to the question on the chart so that the next person will know what question to respond to without looking at the previous answer.
9. Direct students to pass their paper to the person on their right.
10. Each person should have a different paper with a number that corresponds to a different question on the chart.
11. Allow time for the students to read their new question and start the timer.
12. Continue this pattern until each paper has been passed to each student.
13. After everyone has responded to all of the questions, allow time for verbal discussion of the answers. Read the first question and have the person with all of the answers to that question read the responses aloud. Encourage students to discuss, comment, question, and offer compliments to the speakers about their different viewpoints.

106

How do I assess students in literature circles?

SECTION 5

Traditional Assessment Strategies

Traditionally, teachers have assessed student achievement based on their knowledge of specific skills and concepts. These practices primarily key in on only the first three levels of Bloom's Taxonomy: Knowledge, Comprehension, and Application. This stops short of assessing a student's understanding of the text in relationship to their experiences, the world around them, and other texts. Characters, main idea, setting, and sequencing of events are the basic areas that are assessed in literature. These concepts are void of the breadth and depth of assessing understanding that is truly needed to fully comprehend, analyze, and evaluate what students learn from their reading.

It is essential that lesson plans in literature circles and all areas of the curriculum indicate an alignment between instruction and assessment. With this, the teacher is assured that what is being taught in the classroom is also what is reflected in the assessment of students. Furthermore, it is the assessment practices that drive the direction of future lessons.

Literature circles can be assessed on many different levels. Because literature circles encourage students to go beyond the text and make connections to themselves, others, and the world around them, assessments should do the same. Furthermore, the author's purpose and underlying character motivations are also issues shared in literature circle discussions that can be assessed. The assessment should evidence the student's participation in group discussions as well as the general comprehension of the text.

Role sheets can be assessed on effort and/or quality. The teacher, depending on the grading system used in the classroom or school system, should determine the point value that is assigned to each role. This point system may seem too subjective on the part of the teacher. However, a more objective system can be employed if necessary when grading for understanding. There may be times when sheets are collected and points awarded just for completing the role. This is typically done when roles are first introduced. Role sheets should never be used as the only assessment tool when evaluating student achievement.

Alternative Assessment

The complexity of literature circles dictates the need for something other than traditional assessment. Alternative assessments don't always generate a neat number percentage that can be plugged into a grading scale for a letter grade to be spit out. This type of assessment requires planning to reflect what is really being taught in literature circles. Observations, anecdotal records, project rubrics, and student self-assessment rubrics are some forms of alternative assessment that lend themselves to the nature of literature circles.

This is not to say that traditional assessment should be thrown out the window. Instead, a balance can be reached between the need for assessing basic skills and comprehension and assessing the depth of understanding as well as the processes students use to achieve a particular level of thinking. Assessment of literature circles by their very nature should include the student as well as others in the process. It should allow for multiple viewpoints, interpretations, and divergent thinking that is encouraged in literature circle discussions. Again, all assessment should be relevant, meaningful, reflect classroom instruction and expectations, and be used to drive future instruction.

Student Conferences

There may be times when it is necessary to assess a student on an individual basis. One-on-one assessments in the form of individual conferences are useful when assessing comprehension such as retelling events in sequence; making connections to self, others, or other text; the ability to summarize the text with a main idea and details; making predictions; and making inferences. Information regarding a student's ability to utilize common reading strategies such as self-corrections, using context clues, and rereading can aid the teacher when planning for individual needs and mini-lessons. Fluency and oral expression can be observed while the students are in the group setting, but in a conference the teacher can get a longer reading sample without disruptions. While listening to the student read orally, the teacher should note if the student repeats words or phrases, reads smoothly or in a more choppy word-by-word manner, and uses expression as opposed to a monotone voice. On the following page is a sample conference form used during one-on-one reading conferences with students.

Comprehension Conference

Student _____ Date _____

Title of Book _____ Genre_____

For Narrative Text

Teacher: What has happened in the story so far?

Characters: _____

Setting: _____

Problems: _____

Events:_____

Solutions: _____

For Informational Text

Teacher: What are you learning about? Share some information with me.

_____

_____

_____

For All Text

Teacher: Start reading where you left off while I listen. Keep reading until I stop you to ask some questions.

Text Level: _____ Easy _____ Just Right _____ Challenging

Circle a 1, 2, or 3 depending on observations of oral reading.

	Fluency		Self-Monitoring		Oral Expression
1	Repeats words and phrases many times	1	Has many miscues that are not self-corrected	1	Monotone reader, very little oral expression
2	Fairly fluent, word by word at times	2	Uses strategies to correct miscues	2	Reads with some expression
3	Reads fluently, in meaningful chunks	3	Has very few or no miscues	3	Strong oral expression

Teacher Comments: _____

110

Observations and Anecdotal Records

Observations of individuals and groups of students can offer a wealth of information on how a student interacts with others and the level of understanding he or she has of the text. By eavesdropping on student group discussions, the teacher can take notes on the predetermined purpose of the literature lesson. More often than not, the teacher makes notes of the content of the discussion, cooperation of group members, and the process the group is following.

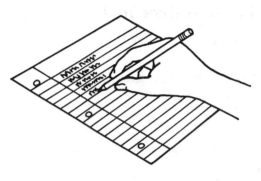

Observations by the teacher should be recorded on the spot. This is easily achieved when carrying a clipboard with paper or with a sheet of blank labels. Notes regarding group or individual behavior and understanding can be jotted down quickly and dated. Some teachers share the notes with students the day of the observation to provide immediate feedback and to guide personal or group goal setting for future lessons.

Anecdotal notes should be brief in nature yet capture the essence of the observation. Brevity will allow for many notes to be taken for a number of students over a short period of time. Areas of observation may include strategies used, language development, social skills and abilities, learning styles, and attitudes.

Strategies

Strategies used are only one area of focus while performing an observation. The obvious strategy to note would be the strategy being emphasized in recent lessons (relating text to self, discussing author purpose, predicting, etc.). Strategies being observed will greatly depend on the level and ability of the students, the type of text that is being presented, the curriculum, and the specific needs of individual students. Questions to keep in mind when observing for the effective use of strategies may include the following:

- Are the students using the strategy correctly?

- Do they demonstrate an understanding and the proper applications of the mini-lessons provided for the strategy?

- Are further re-teaching or enrichment activities needed as evidenced by the students' application of the skills?

Observations and Anecdotal Records (cont.)

Oral Language Skills

Oral language skills are needed in order for students to offer insight and question the views of others in the group. Even students with limited language skills can benefit from the open discussion offered in a literature circle setting. Success for this student would depend on the diversity of language skills of others within the group. Effectively organizing and verbalizing ideas, questioning, and commenting on the discourse of others are areas to note when taking anecdotal records on language skills. Questions to keep in mind when making notes of a student's language skills may include the following:

- At what level did the student enter the group?
- Has the student make any noticeable improvements or declines in language skills?
- What prompts this student to interact more?
- Is the make-up of the group affecting the student's ability to achieve in this area?

In some cases, it may be beneficial to seek the assistance of a neutral observer or the knowledge of a speech and language professional in the building.

Social Skills

Social skills and abilities include the student's ability to follow the protocol and procedures set forth prior to implementing literature circles. This may include being on time, waiting one's turn, sharing appropriate information, being a leader of the group versus being very passive, and understanding his or her role in the overall success of the group. Questions for the teacher to keep in mind may include the following:

- Is the student interacting with the group on a regular basis?
- Is the student taking control of the group so that others become passive, or vice versa?
- Is the student contributing useful and insightful information that is appropriate to the assignment?

Individual Learning Styles

Making observations on individual learning styles can be a very helpful tool when assessing students and planning future lessons. All individuals have their own unique way of learning and interacting with others. Not only should the teacher make note of what learning styles work for the student but also the areas that may need more attention. Instruction can be directed at showcasing a student's strengths to further understanding while weaknesses can be improved to develop a well-rounded approach for the student to make meaning of the lessons. Questions to keep in mind may include the following:

- Does the student prefer to work alone or with a group?
- Are visual aides, auditory input, or kinesthetic stimuli the most effective method for the student to understand information?
- How does the student best display his or her understanding of information?

112

Observations and Anecdotal Records *(cont.)*

Attitudes

As the old adage goes, "Attitude is everything." Because of various learning styles, personalities, ability levels, and personal experiences of the student, attitudes toward literature circles, group work, or reading in general will also vary. Remember, students generally are not familiar with the self-directed style of literature circles. This change in classroom design may affect their attitude and approach to the lessons. It is important for students to feel comfortable and safe sharing their experiences, insights, and viewpoints without being ridiculed by their peers. Taking time when doing Class Read Aloud literature circles and Small Groups (Same Book) literature circles as discussed in Section 2 may help ease the transition to this type of learning. Attitudes of students do not change overnight. Taking anecdotal records that make note of even subtle changes in a student's attitude are important to the overall development of the student. Questions to keep in mind may include the following:

- Does the student value the opinions and viewpoints of others?

- Does the student share in the discussions freely?

- Is independent work completed that may determine the effectiveness of the group as a whole?

Conclusion

Whether done with a clipboard and paper, sticky labels, or with a specific checklist, anecdotal notes can provide a wealth of information from the development of understanding to the attitudes of individuals. Students can be involved in the evaluation process by helping to develop expectations and by setting personal and group goals reflective of the needs on anecdotal records shared by the teacher. Anecdotal notes of a positive nature that are shared with students may help improve attitudes and confidence. It is the teacher's responsibility to determine the skills needed, to set the stage for group effectiveness, and to assess student progress to determine future lessons. Anecdotal records are a window to the student's use of strategies, comprehension, language development, social skills, learning styles, and attitudes— not to mention the effectiveness of classroom management, curricular instruction, and assessment of students. On the following page is a sample form for recording anecdotal records. When using this format, it is suggested that one sheet be used per student to show a running record of progress. New sheets can be started for each unit, grading period, or on an as-needed basis. The class set of these forms can be kept in a three-ring binder. If using labels, they can be affixed to a student-designated sheet in a three-ring binder, into individual folders, or placed in group folders for group comments.

Anecdotal Notes Record Sheet

Date	Strengths	Things to Work On	Progress Seen

Rubrics and Self- and Group Assessments

Traditionally, the teacher is the only one to assess students. The teacher instructs the lesson, the students complete the assignments and prepare for the test, and the teacher has the final say in the progress of students. However, students can learn a lot about themselves, their learning style, and their strengths and weaknesses when given the opportunity to reflect on their work as an individual and as part of a group. They can reflect on their level of participation and the strategies they use during the reading and writing process. Since this style of assessment may be new to the teacher or the students, it is recommended that the teacher start with a more structured approach and then move to a more open-ended approach when the students are ready.

Structured Self-Assessment

A structured self-assessment tool may be a checklist that each student completes. On page 117 is a more structured checklist that a teacher may use with students for self-assessment. The checklist may have a series of questions predetermined by the teacher that matches with the goals and focus of the lessons, the needs of the group, or of the individual. For a younger group of students, responses could be recorded by circling happy or sad faces. However, for the more mature class, a self-evaluation form can be done by marking "Yes" or "No" responses or by students rating themselves on a number scale. Students should be encouraged to assess themselves in such areas as participation in their group, cooperation, strengths, weaknesses, and understanding.

Open-Ended Assessment

Open-ended self-evaluation tools may be completed as a journal entry or a short answer form. With open-ended self-assessments, the students are not given areas on which to reflect. Instead, they are asked to complete statements like the following:

- I think my level of participation today was . . .

- My participation was at this level because . . .

- Today I did well with . . .

- I could have been better in group today if I would have . . .

- I really enjoyed . . .

- I am still a little confused about . . .

These open-ended journal entries are not graded but rather provide the students an opportunity to monitor themselves and set goals for future groups.

Rubrics and Self- and Group Assessments (cont.)

One-on-One Assessment

One-on-one interviews or conferences are an excellent time to discuss self-evaluations with the student and even compare their responses to assessments or anecdotal records that have been kept by the teacher. The results of both assessments should be used by the student to set personal goals for improvement. This could be an area that the teacher then focuses on while doing anecdotal records.

Student-Generated Assessment

Another approach to student involvement in the evaluation process would be to get them involved in the creation of the evaluation tool such as a rubric. Given the areas that are to be evaluated, allow the students to help generate the criteria needed to achieve each point level. Samples of rubrics can be seen in the section on Sharing Showcases (page 85) and Reader Response and Dialogue Entry journals (page 102). If necessary, a sample of acceptable and unacceptable work can be shared with students to guide them toward the right expectations at each level. When students are involved in the assessment process either through self-evaluation checklists or the creation of rubric criteria, they take ownership in the tool, have a better understanding of what is expected of them, and are more likely to take pride in their work.

Group Assessment

Groups should also be given the opportunity to assess how they work together and what needs to be improved upon to strengthen the dynamics of the group as a whole. The Literature Circle's Daily Report on page 118 is one example of how a group can assess themselves. It may be necessary for the teacher to specify the group member that is responsible for completing the form each time.

For groups to succeed at the tasks assigned to them, all members of the group must take an active role. On rare occasions a student may not be able to cooperate with other members of the group or may not complete assignments on time for the benefit of the group. Teachers are encouraged to follow any classroom management plan that is in place for their classroom. However, there may be times when working alone would be the best for both the group and the difficult student. Because a literature circle relies heavily on the interaction of others, the student that is pulled from the group will not have that opportunity. Instead, this student might be required to complete chapter summaries (pages 119 and 120) in place of role sheets and participating in the group. This can be an effective way to encourage participation in future literature circles.

Individual Rating Report

Name_____

Group Name _____

Book _____

Date_____

Respond to each prompt to reflect how you did in class.
- Mark a **1** if you did the very best you could.
- Mark a **2** if you did okay but could have done better.
- Mark a **3** for areas that need improvement.

Skill	1	2	3
I was responsible and brought my book to class.			
My role sheet was finished and done neatly.			
I encouraged others to share during group.			
I sat facing the group and ready to participate.			
I shared during group time by building on the ideas of others.			
When needed, I tried to keep the group on-task and focused on the ideas at hand.			
My body language demonstrated good listening skills.			

Things I learned from my group today:_____

_____

_____

Things I still have questions about: _____

_____

_____

Something I will try to improve on next time: _____

_____

_____

Teacher comments: _____

_____

_____

Literature Circle's Daily Report

Group Name _____

Book _____

Date _____

List the names of each member of the group for the day and place a
check to indicate that they had their book with them and their assignment completed.

Group Member's Name	Have Book	Assignment Done
_____	_____	_____
_____	_____	_____
_____	_____	_____
_____	_____	_____
_____	_____	_____
_____	_____	_____

Today's Accomplishments: _____
_____
_____
_____

Areas We Could Improve On: _____
_____
_____
_____

Teachers Comments: _____
_____
_____
_____
_____

Chapter Reviews

Name_____

Book _____

After every chapter, stop and fill out a chapter review. You should
create the title of the chapter based on the main idea of the chapter.
Your summary should have the main events in order. Remember to include the following:
Who? (character names), Did What? (actions), When? and Where? (setting).

Chapter: _____ Pages: _____ Title (Main Idea): _____

Summary: _____

_____

_____

_____

_____

_____

_____

_____

_____

Chapter: _____ Pages: _____ Title (Main Idea): _____

Summary: _____

_____

_____

_____

_____

_____

_____

_____

Chapter Reviews *(cont.)*

Chapter: _____ Pages: _____ Title (Main Idea): _____

Summary: _____

_____

_____

_____

_____

_____

_____

Chapter: _____ Pages: _____ Title (Main Idea): _____

Summary: _____

_____

_____

_____

_____

_____

_____

Chapter: _____ Pages: _____ Title (Main Idea): _____

Summary: _____

_____

_____

_____

_____

_____

120

What are my resources?

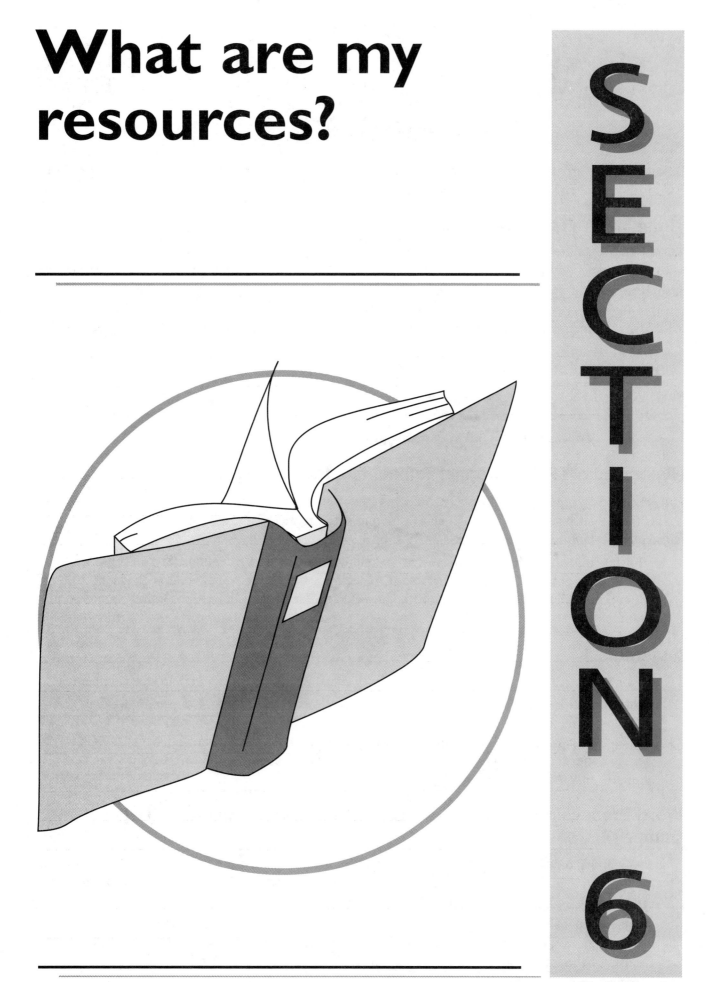

SECTION 6

Software

Below are software resources for literature extensions. A brief explanation of the software is provided. Also listed are the roles that each software program can be used with.

TimeLiner™ (Tom Snyder)

This program allows the students to set up time lines in several different formats. It will also display information in an outline, bulleted, or traditional banner form. Students could create time lines for several sections of the book and then merge them into one as a culminating project. If reading a realistic fiction, for example, students can merge a time line of the book to time lines of that era.

- **Roles:** Timeliner, Scene Setter, Action Plot-O-Graph, A Time of Change, Circle Sequencer

Teacher Spelling Toolkit™ (MECC)

Students can use this program to input and save word lists from their reading. Then, a wide variety of puzzles and practice activities can be generated for personal, group, or whole class use.

- **Roles:** Perfect Puzzler, Word Wizards, Word Webs

HyperStudio® (Roger Wagner Publishing, Inc.)

HyperStudio is a presentation program. Students can use this in a linear fashion to show sequence of events from their reading or in a nonlinear fashion to show connections between characters, events, cause/effect relationships, other books, movies, or the students' own lives.

- **Roles:** Illustrator, Memory Maker, Read-Aloud Master, Poetic Perceptions, Sequencer, Map Matters, A Sense of Character, Character Connections, Character Web, Circle Sequencer, Connection Maker, Dream Weaver, Efficient Effector, Meeting of the Minds, Point/Counterpoint, Summarizer

Inspiration®

Inspiration offers graphic organizers to help students visualize connections and map story elements.

- **Roles:** Advice Columnist, Word Webs, Summarizer, Character Profile, Connection Maker, Efficient Effector, Commentator, Dream Weaver, News Reporter, Read-Aloud Master, Poetic Perceptions, Problem Solver, Scene Setter, Map Matters, A Time of Change, Character Web, Circle Sequencer, Connection Maker, Emotional Events, Meeting of the Minds, New Narrator, Point/Counterpoint, Sensational Sequels, Trait Tracker

Word-Processing Programs (Microsoft® Word and Student Writing Center™)

Students who have difficulty completing paper-and-pencil tasks can use a word-processing program. Most word-processing programs feature spell-checkers, multiple fonts, dictionaries, and thesauruses.

- **Roles:** Advice Columnist, A Time of Change, Commentator, Connection Maker, Discussion Leader, Dream Weaver, Emotional Events, Fortune Teller, Meeting of the Minds, New Narrator, News Reporter, Read-Aloud Master, Poetic Perceptions, Point/Counterpoint, Problem Solver, Sensational Sequels, Summarizer, Trait Tracker, "Wanted!" Poster, Word Wizard

Web Sites

Below is a plethora of Web sites to choose from to gain access to information that will enhance your literature lessons.

The Children's Literature Web Guide

http://www.acs.ucalgary.ca/~dkbrown/

Created by David K. Brown, a librarian, The Children's Literature Web Guide has been in existence since 1998. This site is a compilation of Internet resources related to literature. A list of book awards pulled from print materials and other Internet sites is available. It also features a message board for discussions with other avid readers. Most links on this site were actually recommended by an array of parents, writers, teachers, librarians and even kids.

Amazon Books

http://www.amazon.com

Amazon Books is a commercial site. However, it offers an easy way to search book titles according to genre, age, or interests. On the first screen, click on the BOOKS tab at the top of the page, then click on Children's Books in the left margin.

The Author Corner

http://www.carr.org/authco/

The Author Corner is a great way to research authors for a book study in any curriculum. Click on Other Authors to access links to a Children's Picture Book Database at Miami University or the About Guide to Kids' Books. This link provides lists and links by genre or age appropriate books, as well as links for teachers and parents. The purpose of The Reading Corner link on the main page is to provide children ages two through eight with book reviews. Each category links to a page that is organized alphabetically by the author's last name.

Author Studies

http://www2.scholastic.com/teachers/authorsandbooks/authorstudies/authorstudies.jhtml

The author index on this page lists authors alphabetically by last name for easy searching. Each author page provides a biography and a link to a list of books by that author. This site would be great for comparisons of authors' writing styles and genre studies. The main page also provides a link that would support writing activities that compliment any reading program. Students can review writing tips from their favorite authors in areas such as poetry, biographies, folktales, and fairytales. Students can also participate online in a writer's workshop, as well as publish their work on the Web.

Web Sites (cont.)

The Children's Book Forum

http://faldo.atmos.uiuc.edu/BOOKREVIEW/

Building Rainbows is a site that offers an endless array of book reviews by title. Readers of any age can submit a book review to be posted on the Web site. Submissions include ratings on the overall book and the illustrations. Teachers beware—student entries are posted as received and are not edited for correct spelling or grammar. This would be a great way to provide purpose for student readings and allow them to get insight on a book they may consider reading. Book reviews that are submitted must follow some general guidelines. The link How to Write a Good Book Review shares tips for readers interested in submitting a review.

Just for Kids Who Love Books

http://www.alanbrown.com

This site is kept up-to-date by Alan L. Brown, a retired teacher and librarian in Toronto, Canada. This is a very kid-friendly site that is easy to navigate, easy to read, and very colorful. Click on any book title on the home page to go to a site dedicated to that book. Author links go to informational pages about the author or directly to the author's Web page if one is available. Students can submit general comments or book reviews that will stay posted for 180 days.

Author and Illustrator Pages

http://falcon.jmu.edu/~ramseyil/biochildhome.htm

This is The Internet School Library Media Center's index to author and illustrator Internet sites. It offers literature-related curriculum sites for teachers, school librarians, parents, and students. Biographies, autobiographies, name pronunciation keys, and author birthdays are a few of the features offered at this site. Teachers will find helpful lesson guides that are correlated with Language Arts Reading Standards.

Authors and Illustrators on the Web

http://www.acs.ucalgary.ca/~dkbrown/authors.html

This site offers quick links to authors' Web sites. It is very user friendly and easy to read with the authors' names highlighted and listed in alphabetical order. The button for Other Sources provides links to information about series books, folktales, and author information on school visits and Internet chat rooms.

124

Web Sites *(cont.)*

Aaron Shepard's Reader's Theater Page

http://www.aaronshep.com/rt/

Reader's Theater is a fantastic way for students to share literary works without a lot of fuss. A standard literary forum, Reader's Theater is popular on college campuses and has made its way into the K–12 classrooms. With minimal memorization required and little or no props or costumes, this is an easy way to get students involved in literature across the curriculum. The site offers tips for teachers, as well as practice sheets for students to write their own scripts.

Carol Hurst's Children's Literature Site

http://www.carolhurst.com/

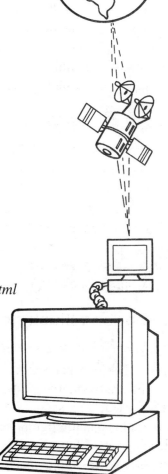

Carol Hurst's site is a wonderful teacher resource. This site has links for books organized by title, author, or grade level. She also includes a vast array of professional information on reading, writing, whole language, math, and social studies, as well as links for other curriculum areas. Her newsletters highlight authors, featured books, or subject areas. You can even view and register for workshops that Carol is presenting.

Selected Children's Literature Special Collection

http://scils.rutgers.edu/%7Ekvander/HistoryofChildLit/specialcollections.html

The School of Communication, Information, and Library Studies presents this Web page. It was created in 1995 and is maintained regularly. The site offers links to online literary collections, such as Center for the Study of Books in Spanish for Children and Adolescents, Ezra Jack Keats Exhibition, and World of the Child: Two Hundred Years of Children's Books, University of Delaware Library.

Fairrosa Cyber Library

http://www.fairrosa.info/

This Web site has a discussion board, reading room, archive of literature, and a reference shelf with links to authors and illustrators and articles and reviews. The reading room has excerpts from classic popular books like *The Velveteen Rabbit* by Margery Williams Bianco. Some even have the entire electronic version of the book. The discussion board and the archives have intriguing conversations on literature-related topics for the teacher. Some recent topics included Allusions in Children's Books and Multiculturalism. There are even discussions on specific book titles.

Web Sites (cont.)

Internet Public Library Youth Division

http://www.ipl.org/cgi-bin/youth/youth.out.pl?sub=rzn0000

This is basically a text-only site, but it has many appropriate links for student use. Students can find links to electronic books and books in Spanish, French, and Braille. There is an endless amount of links to other sites that feature authors in other countries, electronic storytelling using real audio, and even a link that allows children to create their own Wacky Web Tales.

Graphic Organizers

http://www.graphic.org/

Graphic organizers are used to aid students in making sense of what they have read or of what they may want to write about. On the main page, click on GO References and Hotlinks in the left column. Then select Graphic Organizers in Secondary Schools. This will take you to links and samples of graphic organizers. There are more valuable links under More Examples, Brainstorming Strategies, and Mind Mapping.

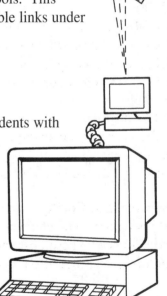

Inspiration®

http://www.engagingminds.com/inspiration/

Inspiration is just one of many computer software packages available to aid students with graphic organizing. This commercial site shares information about *Inspiration* and the elementary version, *Kidspiration*™.

Suite University

http://www.suite101.com/article.cfm/reading/29130
http://www.suite101.com/article.cfm/reading/25008

This is mainly a professional reference for teachers and parents. The two addresses above offer articles about teaching reading. Both addresses have numerous links to related sites, such as Reading Tips, Interactive Web Units, and links to specific school reading programs.

Learning to Read: Resources for Language Arts and Reading Research

http://toread.com/

This is a user-friendly site for teachers and parents about the reading process. This site acts as a clearinghouse for information on Balanced Literacy Programs, Interesting Research, Interactive Lessons, and Professional Organizations and Publications.

Themes and Recommended Book Lists

These themes and lists represent only a sample of possibilities for use in the classroom. In order to capture the interest of this grade level, all of these books listed have young adolescents as the main characters. It is suggested that teachers create a list of themes and books that best complement his or her curriculum and the needs of the students.

Notice that the same author wrote several books in each list. This lends itself to author study in the classroom and for students to develop a taste for the type of writing they prefer. It is also suggested that a book list include award-winning books such as the Newbery Award books.

The first theme "Awareness of Self and Others" is typically realistic fiction books that allow students to learn to be aware of others and to reflect on personal values. These books deal with relationships—personal and interpersonal issues, such as divorce, puberty, and friendship. These books have a strong sense of character development from beginning to end. The characters in these novels are "coming of age."

The theme "Human Rights" includes historical or realistic fiction. The theme deals with characters that have had their human rights violated. For example, in *Roll of Thunder, Hear My Cry* by Mildred D. Taylor, the African-American characters are dealing with racism in the South during the 1930s. Because human rights violations is still an issue in many parts of the world today, historic and realistic fiction can help students form a belief system that will affect their actions toward others.

The "Imagination" theme is one of the more popular themes with students. Saving this unit for the end of the year may be advantageous. These books include fantasy, a taste of science fiction, fairy tales, legends, etc. Students learn to appreciate creativity, learn about the writer's craft and imagination, think outside the box, and get lost in books that are outside the realm of reality.

"Survival and Courage" is a theme that contains realistic fiction books that have a main conflict of man versus nature. The characters demonstrate how to overcome challenges with perseverance, persistence, and patience. These obstacles may include animals, weather, and the physical challenges of surviving outdoors. Through these books student learn to identify the qualities needed to be successful in life.

"Travel Through Time" brings history to life. The focus is on historical events through the eyes of adolescents living during those times. In *Stepping on the Cracks*, the main characters are living in the United States during World War II. One character is hiding a relative that is a deserter of the war, whereas another deals with the death of a brother who fought in the war.

Themes and Recommended Book Lists (cont.)

Awareness of Self and Others

Adler, C.S. *The Lump in the Middle.* Camelot, 1991.

Adler, C.S. *The Once in a While Hero.* Putnam Publishing Group, 1982.

Avi. *Nothing But the Truth: A Documentary Novel* (Newbery Honor, 1992). Flare, 1993.

Avi. *Sun & Spoon.* Puffin, 1998.

Bauer, Joan. *Hope Was Here* (Newbery Honor, 2001). Puffin, 2002.

Bauer, Joan. *Rules of the Road.* Puffin, 2000.

Bauer, Marion Dane. *On My Honor* (Newbery Honor, 1987). Yearling Books, 1987.

Bennett, Cherie. *Searching for David's Heart.* Econo-Clad Books, 1999.

Bloor, Edward. *Tangerine.* Scholastic Paperbacks, 2001.

Bonham, Frank. *Durango Street.* Puffin, 1999.

Byars, Betsy. *Summer of the Swans* (Newbery Medal, 1971). Viking Press, 1996.

Byars, Betsy. *The Cybil War.* Viking Press, 1990.

Conford, Ellen. *Lenny Kandell, Smart Aleck.* Pocket Books, 1987.

Couloumbis, Audrey. *Getting Near to Baby* (Newbery Honor, 2000). Puffin, 2001.

Creech, Sharon. *Walk Two Moons* (Newbery Medal, 1994). HarperTrophy, 1996.

Creech, Sharon. *The Wanderer* (Newbery Honor, 2001). HarperCollins Juvenille Books, 2000.

DeClements, Barthe. *Sixth Grade Can Really Kill You.* Viking Press, 1991.

DiCamillo, Kate. *Because of Winn-Dixie* (Newbery Honor, 2001). Candlewick Press, 2001.

Fleishman, Paul. *Seedfolks.* HarperTrophy, 2000.

Gantos, Jack. *Joey Pigza Loses Control* (Newbery Honor, 2001). HarperTrophy, 2002.

Gantos, Jack. *Joey Pigza Swallowed the Key.* HarperTrophy, 2000.

Gilson, Jamie. *Do Bananas Chew Gum?* Pocket Books, 1981.

Griffen, Adele. *Sons of Liberty.* Hyperion Press, 1998.

Hahn, Mary Downing. *Daphne's Book.* Camelot, 1995.

Hermes, Patricia. *You Shouldn't Have to Say Good-bye.* Apple, 1994.

Hesse, Karen. *Just Juice.* Scholastic Paperbacks, 1999.

Hesse, Karen. *Phoenix Rising.* Puffin, 1995.

Themes and Recommended Book Lists (cont.)

Awareness of Self and Others (cont.)

Hinton, S.E. *The Outsiders.* Prentice Hall, 1997.

Hinton, S.E. *Tex.* Laureleaf, 1989.

Holm, Jennifer L. *Our Only May Amelia* (Newbery Honor, 2000). HarperTrophy, 2001.

Jones, Ron. *The Acorn People.* Laureleaf, 1996.

Konigsburg, E.L. *From the Mixed-up Files of Mrs. Basil E. Frankweiler* (Newbery Medal, 1968). Yearling Books, 1977.

Konigsburg, E.L. *The View from Saturday* (Newbery Medal, 1997). Scott Foresman, 1998.

Lowry, Lois. *A Summer to Die.* Laureleaf, 1984.

MacLachlan, Patricia. *Baby.* Yearling Books, 1995.

Martin, Ann M. *Inside Out.* Holiday House, 1984.

Miklowitz, Gloria D. *After the Bomb.* Scholastic Paperbacks, 1987.

Park, Barbara. *Mick Harte Was Here.* Random House, 1996.

Paterson, Katherine. *Bridge to Terabithia* (Newbery Medal, 1978). HarperTrophy, 1987.

Paterson, Katherine. *The Great Gilly Hopkins* (Newbery Honor, 1979). HarperTrophy, 1987.

Paulsen, Gary. *Harris and Me: A Summer Remembered.* Yearling Books, 1995.

Paulsen, Gary. *The Winter Room* (Newbery Honor, 1990). Laureleaf, 1998.

Peck, Richard. *Remembering the Good Times.* Laureleaf, 1986.

Philbrick, W.R. and Rodman. *Freak the Mighty.* Scholastic Paperbacks, 2001.

Philbrick, W.R. and Rodman. *Max the Mighty.* Point, 1998.

Roos, Stephen. *The Thirteenth Summer.* Troll Associates, 1992.

Rylant, Cynthia. *A Blue-Eyed Daisy.* Aladdin Paperbacks, 2001.

Rylant, Cynthia. *Missing May* (Newbery Medal, 1993). Yearling Books, 1993.

Sachar, Louis. *Holes* (Newbery Medal, 1999). Yearling Books, 2000.

Smith, Doris Buchanan. *A Taste of Blackberries.* HarperTrophy, 1992.

Smith, Robert Kimmel. *The War with Grandpa.* Yearling Books, 1984.

Spinelli, Jerry. *Crash.* Random House, 1997.

Spinelli, Jerry. *The Library Card.* Apple, 1998.

Spinelli, Jerry. *Maniac Magee* (Newbery Medal, 1991). Little, Brown & Co., 2000.

Spinelli, Jerry. *Wringer* (Newbery Honor). HarperTrophy, 1998.

Strasser, Todd. *Friends Till the End.* Laureleaf, 1983.

Themes and Recommended Book Lists (cont.)

Human Rights

Arrick, Fran. *Chernowitz.* New American Library, 1990.

Avi. *Night Journeys.* Avon, 2000.

Bolden, Tonya. *And Not Afraid to Dare: The Stories of Ten African-American Women.* Scholastic Trade, 1998.

Brooks, Polly Shoyer. *Cleopatra: Goddess of Egypt, Enemy of Rome.* Harpercollin's Children's Books, 1995.

Choi, Sooh Nyui. *Year of Impossible Goodbyes.* Yearling Books, 1993.

Collier, James Lincoln. *War Comes to Willy Freeman.* Yearling Books, 1987.

Curtis, Christoper P. *Bud, Not Buddy* (Newbery Medal, 2000). Yearling Books, 2002.

Curtis, Christopher P. *The Watson's Go to Birmingham* (Newbery Honor, 1996). Bantam Books, 1997.

Filipovic, Zlata. *Zlata's Diary: A Child's Life in Sarajevo.* Penguin, 1995.

Greene, Bette. *The Summer of My German Soldier.* Puffin, 1999.

Hesse, Karen. *Letters from Rifka.* Puffin, 1993.

Ho, Minfong. *The Clay Marble.* Farrar, Straus and Giroux, 1993.

Keehn, Sally M. *I Am Regina.* Puffin, 2001.

Lasky, Kathryn. *The Night Journey.* Econo-Clad Books, 1999.

Lord, Bette Bao. *In the Year of the Boar and Jackie Robinson.* HarperTrophy, 1986.

Lowry, Lois. *Autumn Street.* Yearling Books, 1986.

Marshall, James V. *Walkabout.* Sundance Publishers, 1984.

Matas, Carol. *Daniel's Story.* Scholastic Paperbacks, 1993.

Mohr, Nicholasa. *Going Home.* Puffin, 1999.

Moskin, Marietta D. *I Am Rosemarie.* Replica Books, 2001.

Naidoo, Beverley. *Chain of Fire.* HarperTrophy, 1993.

Naidoo, Beverley. *Journey to Jo'Burg: A South African Story.* HarperTrophy, 1988.

Napoli, Donna Jo. *Stones in Water.* Puffin, 1999.

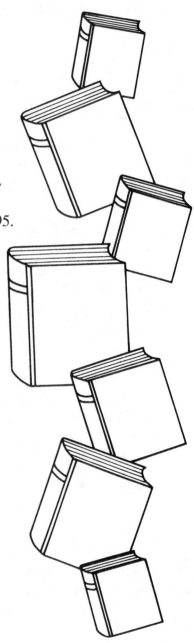

Themes and Recommended Book Lists (cont.)

Human Rights (cont.)

O'Dell, Scott. *Sarah Bishop*. Point, 1991.

O'Dell, Scott. *Thunder Rolling in the Mountains*. Yearling Books, 1993.

Oudia, Sebestyen. *Words by Heart*. Yearling Books, 1997.

Paulsen, Gary. *Nightjohn*. Laureleaf, 1995.

Paulsen, Gary. *Sarny: A Life Remembered*. Laureleaf, 1999.

Pickney, Andrea D. *Hold Fast to Dreams*. Hyperion Press, 1996.

Reiss, Johanna. *The Upstairs Room* (Newbery Honor). HarperTrophy, 1990.

Siegal, Aranka. *Upon the Head of the Goat: A Childhood in Hungary, 1939–1944* (Newbery Honor). Puffin, 1994.

Staples, Suzanne F. *Shabanu: Daughter of the Wind*. Random House Children's Publishers, 1991.

Taylor, Mildred D. *The Friendship* (Coretta Scott King Award). Puffin, 1998.

Taylor, Mildred D. *The Land* (Coretta Scott Award, 2002). Phyllis Fogelman Books, 2001.

Taylor, Mildred D. *Let the Circle Be Unbroken*. Puffin, 1991.

Taylor, Mildred D. *Mississippi Bridge*. Bantam Skylark, 1992.

Taylor, Mildred D. *The Road to Memphis*. Puffin, 1992.

Taylor, Mildred D. *Roll of Thunder, Hear My Cry* (Newbery Medal, 1977). Puffin, 1996.

Taylor, Mildred D. *Song of the Trees*. Skylark, 1996.

Taylor, Mildred D. *The Well: David's Story*. Dial Books for Young Readers, 1995.

Uchida, Yoshiko. *Jar of Dreams*. Aladdin Paperbacks, 1993.

Uchida, Yoshiko. *Journey to Topaz*. Scott Foresman, 1998.

Uchida, Yoshiko. *The Best Bad Thing*. Aladdin Publishing Company, 1986.

Uchida, Yoshiko. *The Happiest Ending*. Margaret McElderry, 1985.

Watkins, Yoko and Jean Fritz. *So Far from the Bamboo Grove*. Beech Tree Books, 1994.

Yep, Laurence. *Dragonwings: Golden Mountain Chronicles, 1903* (Newbery Honor). HarperTrophy, 1989.

Yep, Laurence. *The Star Fisher*. Puffin, 1992.

Themes and Recommended Book Lists (cont.)

Imagination

Adams, Richard. *Watership Down.* Avon, 1999.

Alexander, Lloyd. *The Book of Three.* Yearling Books, 1999.

Avi. *Ereth's Birthday.* HarperTrophy, 2001.

Avi. *Midnight Magic.* Scholastic Paperbacks, 2001.

Avi. *Perloo the Bold.* Scholastic Paperbacks, 1999.

Avi. *Poppy.* Camelot, 1997.

Avi. *Poppy and Rye.* Camelot, 1999.

Avi. *Ragweed.* HarperTrophy, 2000.

Babbit, Natalie. *Tuck Everlasting.* Farrar, Straus and Giroux, 1986.

Barron, T.A. *The Lost Years of Merlin.* Berkley Publishing Group, 1999.

Barron, T.A. *The Seven Songs of Merlin* (The Lost Years of Merlin, Book 2). Berkley Publishing Group, 1997.

Cooper, Susan. *Silver on the Tree* (The Dark Is Rising Sequence). Pocket Books, 1986.

Cooper, Susan. *The Dark is Rising* (Newbery Honor, 1974). Aladdin Paperbacks, 1999.

Cooper, Susan. *The Grey King* (Newbery Medal, 1976). Aladdin Paperbacks, 1999.

Dahl, Roald. *The BFG.* Puffin, 1998.

Dahl, Roald. *Matilda.* Puffin, 1998.

Dahl, Roald. *The Witches.* Puffin, 1998.

Dahl, Roald. *The Wonderful Story of Henry Sugar and Six More.* Puffin, 2000.

Farmer, Nancy. *The Ear, the Eye, and the Arm* (Newbery Honor, 1995). Penguin Putnam Inc., 1995.

Grahame, Kenneth. *The Wind in the Willows.* Aladdin Paperbacks, 1989.

Haddix, Margaret Peterson. *Among the Hidden.* Aladdin Paperbacks, 2000.

Haddix, Margaret Peterson. *Among the Imposters.* Simon & Schuster, 2001.

Haddix, Margaret Peterson. *Running Out of Time.* Aladdin Paperbacks, 1997.

Ibbotson, Eva. *Island of the Aunts.* Puffin, 2001.

Ibbotson, Eva. *The Secret of Platform 13.* Puffin, 1999.

Ibbotson, Eva. *Which Witch?* Puffin, 2000.

Juster, Norton. *The Phantom Tollbooth.* Random House, 1993.

Levine, Gail Carson. *Cinderellis and the Glass Hill* (The Princess Tales Series). HarperCollins Juvenile Books, 2000.

Levine, Gail Carson. *Ella Enchanted* (Newbery Honor, 1998). HarperTrophy, 1998.

Themes and Recommended Book Lists *(cont.)*

Imagination *(cont.)*

Levine, Gail Carson. *The Fairy's Mistake* (The Princess Tales Series). HarperCollins Juvenile Books, 1999.

Levine, Gail Carson. *Princess Sonora and the Long Sleep* (The Princess Tales Series). HarperCollins Juvenile Books, 1999.

Levine, Gail Carson. *The Princess Test* (The Princess Tales Series). HarperCollins Juvenile Books, 1999.

Levine, Gail Carson. *The Wish*. HarperTrophy, 2001.

Lewis, C.S. *The Chronicles of Narnia* (7 books). HarperCollins Juvenile Books, 1994.

Lunn, Janet. *The Root Cellar.* Puffin, 1996.

McCaffrey, Anne. *Dragonsong (1).* Bantam Spectra, 1977.

McCaffrey, Anne. *Dragonsinger (2).* Bantam Books, 1997.

McCaffrey, Anne. *Dragondrums (3).* Bantam Books, 1996.

Norton, Mary. *The Borrowers (1).* Odyssey Classics, 1989.

Norton, Mary. *The Borrowers Avenged (2).* Odyssey Classics, 1990.

O'Brien, Robert C. *Z for Zachariah.* Pocket Books, 1987.

Paulsen, Gary. *The Transall Saga.* Laureleaf, 1999.

Pierce, Tamora. *Briar's Book (Circle of Magic Series, 4).* Point, 2000.

Pierce, Tamora. *Daja's Book (Circle of Magic Series, 3).* Point, 2000.

Pierce, Tamora. *Sandry's Book (Circle of Magic Series, 1).* Point, 1999.

Pierce, Tamora. *Tris's Book (Circle of Magic Series, 2).* Point, 1999.

Pullman, Phillip. *The Golden Compass (His Dark Materials, No. 1).* Del Rey, 1999.

Pullman, Phillip. *The Subtle Knife (His Dark Materials, No. 2).* Del Rey, 1999.

Pullman, Phillip. *The Amber Spyglass (His Dark Materials, No. 3).* Del Rey, 2001.

Pullman, Phillip. *The Firework-Maker's Daughter.* Scholastic Paperbacks, 2001.

Sczieska, Jon. *Time Warp Trio Series.* Puffin, 2001.

Snicket, Lemony. *A Series of Unfortunate Events (9 books).* HarperCollins Juvenile books, 2001.

Sutcliff, Rosemary. *Dragon Slayer.* Viking Press, 1995.

Tolkien, J.R.R. *The Hobbit.* Houghton Mifflin Co., 1973.

Walsh, Jill Paton. *The Green Book.* Farrar, Straus and Giroux, 1986.

Winthrop, Elizabeth. *Battle for the Castle.* Yearling Books, 1999.

Winthrop, Elizabeth. *The Castle in the Attic.* Yearling Books, 1986.

Themes and Recommended Book Lists (cont.)

Survival and Courage

Bauer, Joan. *Backwater.* Puffin, 2000.

Campbell, Eric. *The Place of Lions.* Harcourt, 1995.

Casanova, Mary. *Moose Tracks.* Disney Press, 1997.

Casanova, Mary. *Wolf Shadows.* Hyperion Press, 1999.

DeFelice, Cynthia. *Weasel.* Econo-Clad Books, 1999.

Duey, Kathleen. *Survival! Blizzard (Estes Park, Colorado, 1886).* Aladdin Paperbacks, 1998.

Ellis, Ella Thorp. *Swimming with the Whales.* Juniper, 1996.

Fleischman, Sid. *Jim Ugly.* Yearling Books, 1993.

Gardiner, John Reynolds. *Stone Fox.* HarperTrophy, 1988.

George, Jean Craighead. *Julie of the Wolves* (Newbery Medal, 1973). HarperTrophy, 1974.

George, Jean Craighead. *Missing 'Gator of Gumbo Limbo: An Eco Mystery.* HarperTrophy, 1993.

George, Jean Craighead. *The Cry of the Crow.* HarperTrophy, 1988.

George, Jean Craighead. *My Side of the Mountain* (Newbery Honor, 1960). Scott Foresman, 2000.

George, Jean Craighead. *On the Far Side of the Mountain.* Scott Foresman, 1991.

George, Jean Craighead. *Summer of the Falcon.* HarperTrophy, 1979.

George, Jean Craighead. *The Talking Earth.* HarperTrophy, 1987.

George, Jean Craighead. *Water Sky.* HarperTrophy, 1989.

George, Jean Craighead. *Who Really Killed Cock Robin?: An Ecological Mystery.* HarperCollins Juvenile Books, 1992.

Hill, Kirkpatrick. *Winter Camp.* Puffin, 1995.

Hobbs, Will. *Beardance.* Camelot, 1999.

Hobbs, Will. *Bearstone.* Camelot, 1997.

Hobbs, Will. *Downriver.* Dell Publishing Co., 1996.

Hobbs, Will. *Far North.* Camelot, 1997.

Hobbs, Will. *River Thunder.* Laureleaf, 1999.

Kjelgaard, James Arthur. *Stormy.* Bantam Skylark, 1983.

Themes and Recommended Book Lists *(cont.)*

Survival and Courage *(cont.)*

Moeri, Louise. *Save the Queen of Sheba.* Puffin, 1994.

O'Dell, Scott. *Black Star, Bright Dawn.* Juniper, 1990.

O'Dell, Scott. *Island of the Blue Dolphins* (Newbery Medal, 1961). Scott Foresman, 1987.

O'Dell, Scott. *Sing Down the Moon* (Newbery Honor, 1971). Yearling Books, 1992.

O'Dell, Scott. *Streams to the River, River to the Sea.* Fawcett Books, 1988.

Paulsen, Gary. *Brian's Winter.* Laureleaf, 1998.

Paulsen, Gary. *Dogsong* (Newbery Honor). Pocket Books, 1999.

Paulsen, Gary. *Father Water, Mother Woods: Essays on Fishing and Hunting in the North Woods.* Dell Publishing, 1996.

Paulsen, Gary. *Guts: The True Stories Behind Hatchet and the Brian Books.* Laureleaf, 2002.

Paulsen, Gary. *Hatchet* (Newbery Honor, 1998). Pocket Books, 1999.

Paulsen, Gary. *My Life in Dog Years.* Yearling Books, 1999.

Paulsen, Gary. *The Island.* Laureleaf, 1990.

Paulsen, Gary. *The River.* Yearling Books, 1993.

Paulsen, Gary. *Tracker.* Pocket Books, 1995.

Paulsen, Gary. *Woodsong.* Scott Foresman, 1991.

Smith, Roland. *Jaguar.* Hyperion Press, 1998.

Smith, Roland. *The Last Lobo.* Hyperion Press, 2001.

Smith, Roland. *Thunder Cave.* Disney Press, 1997.

Speare, Elizabeth George. *Calico Captive.* Houghton Mifflin Co., 2001.

Speare, Elizabeth George. *The Sign of the Beaver* (Newbery Honor, 1984). Yearling Books, 1994.

Sperry, Armstrong. *Call It Courage* (Newbery Medal, 1941). Scott Foresman, 1990.

Taylor, Theodore. *The Cay.* Yearling Books, 2002.

Willis, Patricia. *Danger Along the Ohio.* Camelot, 1999.

Themes and Recommended Book Lists (cont.)

Travel Through Time

Angeli, Marguerite de. *The Door in the Wall* (Newbery Medal, 1950). Yearling Books, 1990.

Armstrong, William H. *Sounder* (Newbery Medal, 1970). HarperTrophy, 1969.

Avi. *The True Confessions of Charlotte Doyle* (Newbery Honor, 1991). Avon, 1992.

Conrad, Pam. *Prairie Songs.* HarperTrophy, 1993.

Fleischman, Paul. *The Borning Room.* HarperTrophy, 1993.

Fleischman, Paul. *Bull Run.* HarperTrophy, 1995.

Fleischman, Sid. *The Whipping Boy* (Newbery Medal, 1987). Troll Associates, 1989.

Fleischman, Sid. *Bandit's Moon.* Yearling Books, 2000.

Giff, Patricia Reilly. *Lily's Crossing* (Newbery Honor, 1998). Yearling Books, 1999.

Giff, Patricia Reilly. *Nory Ryan's Song.* Yearling Books, 2002.

Hahn, Mary Downing. *As Ever, Gordy.* Camelot, 2000.

Hahn, Mary Downing. *Following My Own Footsteps.* Camelot, 1998.

Hahn, Mary Downing. *Stepping on the Cracks* (Scott O'Dell Award for Historical Fiction). Camelot, 1992.

Hesse, Karen. *Out of the Dust* (Newbery Medal, 1998). HarperTrophy, 2001.

Hesse, Karen. *Stowaway.* Aladdin Paperbacks, 2002.

Holm, Jennifer L. *Our Only May Amelia* (Newbery Honor, 2000). HarperTrophy, 2001.

Hunt, Irene. *Across Five Aprils* (Newbery Honor, 1965) Berkley Publishing Group, 1987.

Levine, Gail Carson. *Dave at Night.* HarperTrophy, 2001.

Lord, Bette Bao. *In the Year of the Boar and Jackie Robinson.* HarperTrophy, 1986.

Magorian, Michelle. *Good Night, Mr. Tom.* HarperTrophy, 1986.

Patterson, Katherine. *Jip: His Story.* Puffin, 1998.

Patterson, Katherine. *Lyddie.* Puffin, 1994.

Patterson, Katherine. *Park's Quest.* Viking Press, 1989.

Paulsen, Gary. *Harris and Me: A Summer Remembered.* Yearling Books, 1995.

Paulsen, Gary. *Mr. Tucket.* Yearling Books, 1995.

Paulsen, Gary. *The Winter Room* (Newbery Honor, 1989). Laureleaf, 1998.

Peck, Richard. *A Long Way From Chicago* (Newbery Honor, 1999). Puffin, 2000.

Peck, Richard. *A Year Down Yonder* (Newbery Medal, 2001). Dial Books for Young Readers, 2000.

White, Ruth. *Belle Prater's Boy* (Newbery Honor, 1997). Yearling Books, 1998.

Graphic Organizers

Many Different Kinds

Graphic organizers are diagrams, sketches, pictures, clusters, maps, outlines, etc. designed to help students put their thoughts into a logical form in order to clarify concepts or point out relationships between and among them. There are as many graphic organizers as there are people who organize. Some, however, have become more generally accepted than others.

Teachers who are trying to get students to write a paragraph with a main idea and four supporting ideas might draw a picture on the board, depending on their degree of artistic prowess, of an elephant or of a table. The body of the elephant (or the top of the table) is the main idea and the legs are the supporting ideas. The elephant, or the table, stands up best when all the ideas are present. You probably draw items like this all the time. In so doing, you are using graphic organizers. For example:

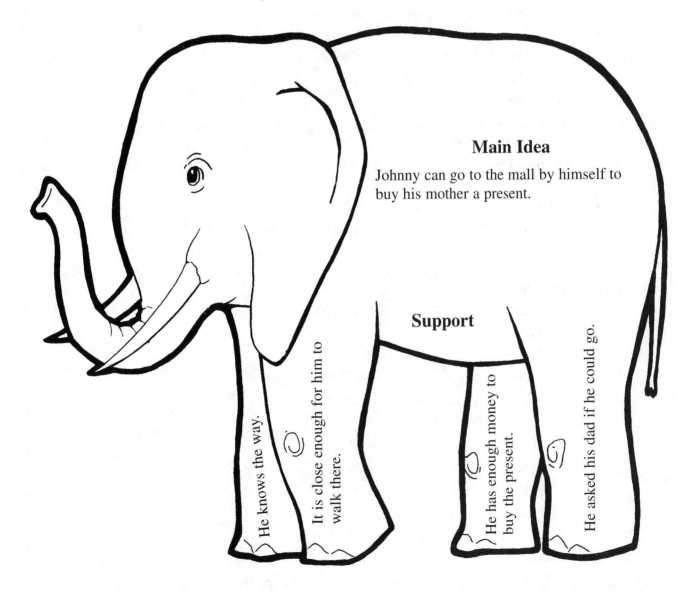

Main Idea

Johnny can go to the mall by himself to buy his mother a present.

Support

He knows the way.

It is close enough for him to walk there.

He has enough money to buy the present.

He asked his dad if he could go.

137

Graphic Organizers (cont.)

Cluster A

This type of graphic organizer places the main idea at its center, with supporting ideas radiating from the main idea.

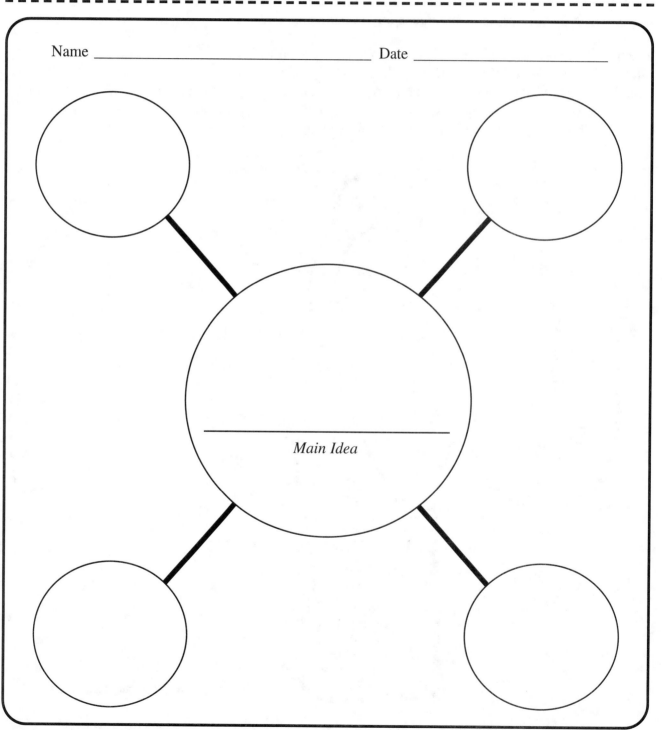

Name _____ Date _____

Main Idea

Graphic Organizers *(cont.)*

Cluster B

This is a variation of a web cluster, with information clustered around the supporting ideas that connect to the main idea.

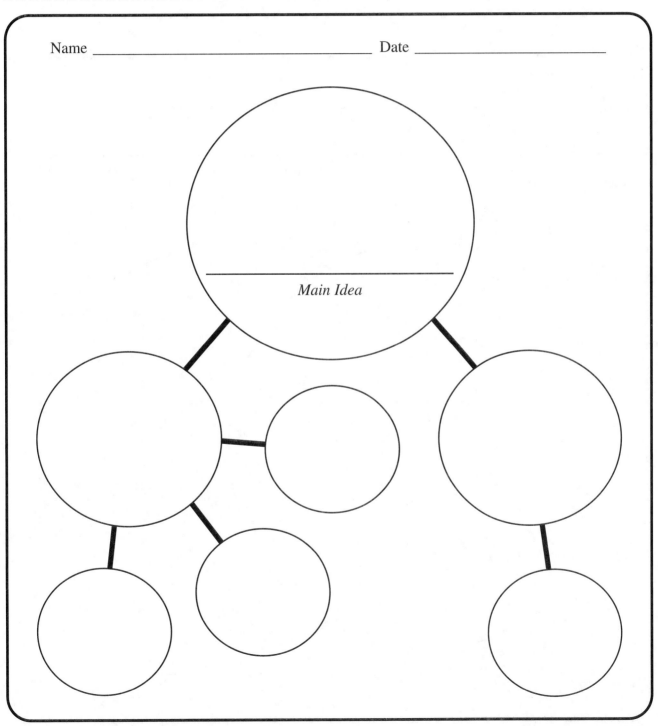

Name _____ Date _____

Main Idea

Graphic Organizers *(cont.)*

Venn Diagram A

A Venn diagram can show students' thought processes as they compare topics, characters, or objects, demonstrating the differences and similarities. Areas where the circles overlap represent qualities in common. Areas of the circles which do not overlap show dissimilar characteristics.

Name _____ Date _____

_____

Subject or Title

Graphic Organizers *(cont.)*

Venn Diagram B

A Venn diagram can show students' thought processes as they compare topics, characters, or objects, demonstrating the differences and similarities. Areas where the circles overlap represent qualities in common. Areas of the circles which do not overlap show dissimilar characteristics. This Venn diagram is drawn to compare and contrast three objects, characters, or topics.

- -

Name _____ Date _____

_____

Subject or Title

Graphic Organizers *(cont.)*

Character Web

A character web is a design of boxes and circles which helps to analyze the basic attributes of a single character and his or her relationship to the book as a whole. A drawing and/or the name of the character goes in the middle box. It is surrounded by circles for specific characteristics such as physical description, personality traits, occupation/special abilities, and relationship to other characters. This is an excellent device to help understand and remember the characters in any story.

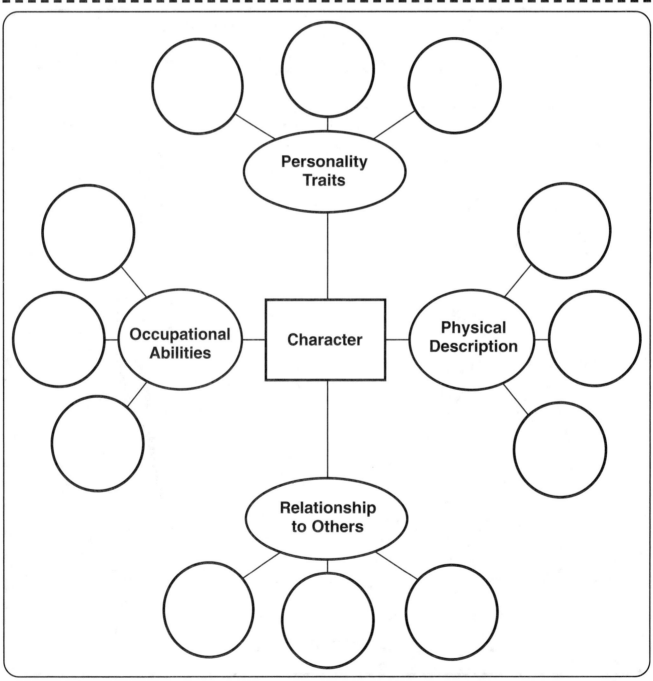

Graphic Organizers *(cont.)*

The Open Mind

Students write and organize their ideas inside the outline of a head, which symbolizes a character's thoughts.

Name _____ Date _____

_____
Character

Bibliography

Beers, K. & B.G. Samuels. *Intofocus: Understanding and Creating Middle School Readers.* Norwood, MA: Christopher-Gordon Publisher, Inc., 1998.

Chambers, A. *Tell Me: Children, Reading, and Talk.* York, ME: Stenhouse Publishers, 1996.

Cunningham, P.M. and R.L. Allington. *Classrooms That Work: They Can All Read and Write.* New York, NY: Longman, 1999.

Daniels, H. *Literature Circles: Voice and Choice in the Student-Centered Classroom.* York, ME: Stenhouse Publishers, 1994.

Daniels, H. and M. Bizar. *Methods That Matter: Six Structures for Best Practice Classrooms.* York, ME: Stenhouse Publishers, 1998.

Deterson, R. and M. Eeds. *Grand Conversations.* New York, NY: Scholastic, 1990.

Harvey, S. and A. Goudvis. *Strategies That Work: Teaching Comprehension to Enhance Understanding.* York, ME: Stenhouse Publishers, 2000.

Moore, D.W., et. al. *Adolescent Literacy: A Position Statement on Adolescent Literacy of the International Reading Association.* Newark, DE: International Reading Association, Inc., 1999.

Keene, E.O. and S. Zimmerman. *Mosaic of Thought: Teaching Reading Comprehension in a Reader's Workshop.* Portsmouth, NH: Heinemann, 1997.

Morretta, T. and M. Ambrosini. *Practical Approaches for Teaching Reading and Writing in Middle Schools.* Newark, DE: International Reading Association Inc., 2000.

Routman, R. *Conversations: Strategies for Teaching, Learning, and Evaluating.* Portsmouth, NH: Heinemann, 2000.

Routman, R. *Invitations: Changing as Teachers and Learners K–12.* Portsmouth, NH: Heinemann, 1991.

Samway, K.D. and G. Whang. *Literature Study Circles in a Multicultural Classroom.* York, ME: Stenhouse Publishers, 1996.

Short, K.G. and K.M. Pierce. *Talking About Books: Creating Literate Communities.* Portsmouth, NH: Heinemann, 1990.